Lecture Notes of the Institute for Computer Sciences, Social Informatics and Telecommunications Engineering 161

More information about this series at http://www.springer.com/series/8197

Carlos Vaz de Carvalho · Paula Escudeiro
António Coelho (Eds.)

Serious Games, Interaction, and Simulation

5th International Conference, SGAMES 2015
Novedrate, Italy, September 16–18, 2015
Revised Selected Papers

Springer

Editors
Carlos Vaz de Carvalho
Instituto Superior de Engenharia do Porto
Porto
Portugal

António Coelho
University of Porto
Porto
Portugal

Paula Escudeiro
Instituto Superior de Engenharia do Porto
Porto
Portugal

ISSN 1867-8211 ISSN 1867-822X (electronic)
Lecture Notes of the Institute for Computer Sciences, Social Informatics and Telecommunications Engineering
ISBN 978-3-319-29059-1 ISBN 978-3-319-29060-7 (eBook)
DOI 10.1007/978-3-319-29060-7

Library of Congress Control Number: 2016934664

Printed on acid-free paper

This Springer imprint is published by Springer Nature
The registered company is Springer International Publishing AG Switzerland

Preface

These proceedings represent the work of researchers participating in GAMES 2015, the 5th International Conference on Serious Games, Interaction and Simulation that took place at e-Campus University, in Novedrate, Italy, during September 16–18, 2015. This conference is a multidisciplinary approach to the presentation of research, theory, application, practice, and validation in the field of serious games for any level and any area. It covers areas such as cognition, psychology, technology-enhanced education, evaluation and assessment, multimedia, and information technology.

The program of SGAMES 2015 was focused on distinct areas from tools and applications to the advancements in core issues of serious games design and development. One of the major applications areas is education: contributions range from gamified approaches towards preventing school leaving, a virtual city model to foster mathematics and science in secondary education students, an exploratory study on the role of chess playing in the teaching of mathematics, another study that investigates to what extent the use of sensitizing techniques can help children design a serious game, the analysis of the relationship between game genres and competence development, and the knowledge improvement of dental students through an online serious game. Another area focused on is accessibility, both for disabled people and elderly people. From a game that aims to make the process of learning sign language easier and enjoyable, or a method for applying the effort of university students to the benefit of Down's syndrome children, to serious games for attention training and cognitive stimulation of the older adults. Another paper proposes new ways of guiding players' actions toward image and video crowdsourcing. Regarding tools, a model-driven authoring framework is proposed as high-level authoring environments for non-technical domains. In the core issues of serious games design and development, the contributions range from dynamic serious games balancing to a preliminary version of a serious game quality model. Beside serious games, gamification is also approached in two papers, from fostering learning engagement toward preventing early school leaving to the integration of building information modeling (BIM) together with the emergent Internet of Things (IoT).

We hope you enjoy these articles and profit from them as much as we did editing them. The quality of the contributions shows tremendous potential for a bright future. See you at SGAMES 2016.

March 2016

Carlos Vaz de Carvalho
Paula Escudeiro
António Coelho

Organization

General Chair

Carlos Vaz de Carvalho — Instituto Superior de Engenharia do Porto, Portugal

TPC Chair

Paula Escudeiro — Instituto Superior de Engenharia do Porto, Portugal

Workshops Chair

Joze Rugelj — University of Ljubljana, Slovenia

Publicity Chair

Martin Sillaots — Tallinn University, Estonia

Sponsorship and Exhibits Chair

Ivan Martinez-Ortiz — Complutense University of Madrid, Spain

Panels Chair

Hariklia Tsalapata — University of Thessaly, Greece

Posters and PhD Track Chair

Gavin Sim — University of Central Lancashire, UK

Publications Chair

Antonio Coelho — University of Porto, Portugal

Web Chair

Antonio Andrade — Virtual Campus Lda., Porto, Portugal

Local Chair

Stefano Za — Universitá degli Studi eCampus, Novedrate (CO), Italy

Conference Manager

Jana Vlnkova — EAI, Slovakia

Contents

Editorial

Carlos Vaz de Carvalho[1(✉)], Paula Escudeiro[1], and António Coelho[2]

[1] Instituto Superior de Engenharia do Porto,
Rua Dr. António Bernardino de Almeida, 431, 4200-072 Porto, Portugal
{cmc,pmo}@isep.ipp.pt

[2] Faculdade de Engenharia da Universidade do Porto,
Rua Dr. Roberto Frias, 4200-072 Porto, Portugal
acoelho@fe.up.pt

Welcome to SGAMES 2015, the 5th International Conference on Serious Games, Interaction and Simulation. This conference is a multidisciplinary approach to the presentation of research, theory, application, practice and validation in the fields of Serious Games, Interaction and Simulation. As such it covers areas like cognition, psychology, technology-enhanced education, evaluation and assessment, multimedia and information technology. It is the place to show and to see new scientific approaches and results from experiments and real-life applications.

1 SGAMES and SEGAN

SGAMES 2015 also marks the beginning of a new era for this conference series. The first four editions of the conference were organized solely under the scope of SEGAN – the Serious Games European Association. This association aims at studying, analyzing and disseminating information about serious games, systematizing the research and application processes, exchanging knowledge, experience and know-how between the different countries, institutions and individuals. SEGAN also aims at identifying and disseminating the best practices in this field, as well as encouraging new actors to participate and use serious games. SEGAN defines future research and development lines, and expects to promote Europe as a center for the development of projects.

The SEGAN association is an already quite large community of practice with more than 1000 participants who regularly contribute with information, news, reviews and opinions. The community is based on social networks and online tools to improve its visibility, to generalize the knowledge and impact about serious games as well as to contribute for their adoption and efficient use. The network has created an online social portal organized in groups of interest that produces annual reports on the design, development and assessment of serious games, and on their use in specific contexts. Furthermore, a repository of products, papers and projects related to serious games has been developed, and reference documents related to the design, development and assessment of serious games are also produced. The social portal, which includes the repository is available at http://seriousgamesnet.eu/community.

C. Vaz de Carvalho et al. (Eds.): SGAMES 2015, LNICST 161, pp. 1–5, 2016.
DOI: 10.1007/978-3-319-29060-7_1

Other available web tools are:

- The network's website at http://seriousgamesnet.eu
- A Facebook group, available at http://www.facebook.com/groups/segan

The network also holds local events on the development of serious games and, as previously mentioned, organized a series of annual conferences and summer schools in Zaragoza (2012), Tallin (2013), Cork (2014), and Tenerife (2015). SGAMES 2015 marks the beginning of a partnership between SEGAN and EAI in the joint organization of the conference. The main subject of the conference is still "serious games," which may be defined as games used for purposes other than mere entertainment.

2 Serious Games

Serious games may be applicable in a wide range of areas such as education, health, training implying dangerous environments or situations, etc. Serious games are particularly useful for education and training purposes. Instead of offering only the traditional paper or online static courses, integrating serious games in the classroom, and their corresponding educational activities at home, may offer immersive and attractive environments in which the users "learn by doing." The users act and learn from their own mistakes in a controlled environment. This method based on attempt and error is a good support for learning, and it is also capable of improving team work, social leadership skills and collaboration.

3 The Conference

The program of SGAMES 2015 is focused on distinct areas from tools and applications to the advancements in core issues of serious games design and development. In the core issues of serious games design and development the contributions range from dynamic serious games balancing to a preliminary version of a serious game quality model. Vaz de Carvalho presents Dynamic Serious Games Balancing a way to raise and keep the user's interest in a game through specific, user-adapted mechanisms that are necessary to keep his/her interest and motivation. Dynamic game balancing (DGB) is the process of changing game parameters in real-time, according to the users' detected ability, in order to provide him/her with a tight fit challenge (neither too easy nor too difficult).

García-Mundo et al. introduce a preliminary version of a Serious Game Quality Model (QSGame-Model), present an example of the application of this model and outline the future empirical studies necessary to refine and validate the model.

But, like previously mentioned, one of the major applications areas is Education: several contributions range from gamified approaches towards preventing school leaving, a virtual city model to foster Mathematics and Science in Secondary education students, an exploratory study on the role of chess playing in the teaching of mathematics, another study that investigates to what extent the use of sensitizing techniques can help children design a serious game, the analysis of the relation between game genres and competence development and the knowledge Improvement of dental students through an online serious game.

Sim et al. describe a study to investigate to what extent the use of sensitizing techniques can help children design a serious game for a surrogate population and understand what children can contribute to the general development of serious games and to the specifics of thinking about other populations.

Heidmann et al. address the issue of secondary education students often struggling with Mathematics and Sciences and presents a game-based Problem-Based Learning approach. This work, named eCity, aims at creating a Virtual Learning Environment platform in the form of a city building simulator, in which students, often digital native, will feel at ease and encouraged to solve the practical engineering scenarios they will face.

Kakoma and Apostolos undertook a study into the role that chess plays in the learning of Mathematics. The study offers some new insights into the role that chess plays in the teaching and learning of mathematics. Preliminary results show that there is a correlation between playing chess and the learning of Mathematics.

Baptista et al. addresses the issue of in-game certification of skills and competences considering that the effectiveness of game-based training is directly related to the success on how the challenges promote the acquisition of skills. In the article a study is presented identifying the most appropriate game genres to develop specific skills and competences.

Sipiyaruk et al. present a serious game for Dental Public Health (DPH), developed to support students in designing health promotion programmes. Based on the evaluation data from an initial pilot study there was evidence that this game had the potential to be a global learning tool.

Rugelj presents a study on the use of serious computer games design for active learning in teacher education. Active learning is a pedagogical method that focuses the responsibility of learning on learners. They engage in activities, such as reading, writing, discussion, or problem solving that promote analysis, synthesis, and evaluation of class content. There is a convergence between the core elements of good serious game design and the characteristics of productive learning. Another link between games and learning is formative feedback as a critical part of any learning effort and a key component in game design that adjusts challenges.

Another area focused is accessibility, both for disabled people and elderly peoples. From a game that aims to make the process of learning sign language easier and enjoyable, or a method for applying the effort of university students to the benefit of Down's syndrome children, to serious games for attention training and cognitive stimulation of the older adults.

Cardoso et al. propose a method for applying the effort and enthusiasm of final year students from technology universities in existing social needs like the care for children with Down syndrome, Deafness or Autism Spectrum Disorders through games' development.

Escudeiro et al. present a game developed within the Virtual sign project that aims to make the process of learning sign language easier and enjoyable. In the game the player can control an avatar and interact with several objects and non-player characters in order to obtain signs. The player then has to perform the gesture himself/herself. This improves the interactivity and makes the game more interesting and motivating.

Alves et al. present a proposal to stimulate cognitively adults through Serious Games, helping them to develop strategies and maintaining independency in their daily life activities.

Ku et al. present the design and study of a Serious Game for attention training of the older adults. They designed a parameterizable serious game on tablet computer to study how such a system can improve the attention of the older adults. The experimental results show that some cognitive abilities of the participants can be significantly improved, and most of the subjects are willing to continue to play the game after the experiments.

Another paper proposes new ways of guiding players' actions towards image and video crowdsourcing. Simões et al. outline some basic mechanics in serious games that can be explored for the purpose of data collection and they describe new ways of guiding players' actions towards the purpose of image and video crowdsourcing. This way the access to large-scale imagery datasets can be significantly improved namely for applications in 3D modelling, augmented reality, infrastructure inspection, urban planning, etc.

Regarding tools, a model-driven authoring framework is proposed as high-level authoring environments for non-technical domain. Van Hoecke et al. present a model-driven authoring framework for high-level authoring environments and support for non-technical domain experts to create custom serious games. Through model-driven authoring, non-technical people can manipulate the 3D visuals of their serious game, model the scenarios of the game, and even easily add non-linear narrative to the game.

Besides Serious Games, Gamification is also approached in several papers, from fostering learning engagement towards preventing early school leaving to the integration of Building Information Modeling (BIM) together with the emergent Internet of Things (IoT). Tsalapatas et al. present a gamified community for fostering learning engagement and preventing early school leaving. Their work aims at strengthening the ties of school networks aiming at preventing ESL risk factors to set root in a learner's life through early interventions that start in primary school. This is pursued through a gamified school community and supporting gamified complementary to school curricula learning activities that aim at fostering engagement of parents, teachers, and learners.

Steven Rowland then explores how gamification can provide the platform for this purpose fostering the creation of a testable and persistent virtual building via gaming technology that combines both BIM and IoT. The author discusses the features of each subject area in brief, and points towards the advantages and challenges of integration via gaming technology.

4 Closing

SGAMES 2015 was an excellent opportunity to be in contact with the most recent research and developments in the Serious Games domain. The quality of the contributions and of the discussions clearly showed tremendous potential for collaboration and evolution which we expect will continue in the next years. SGAMES 2016 will definitely confirm this trend and, besides the strengthening of the current research, we will be able to see new areas of application of Serious Games.

Co-locating SGAMES with e-LEOT also made all the sense and allowed for a very profitable synergy and gathering of expertise between the participants in both events. Therefore next year we will continue this partnership.

So you have reasons to meet us and we look forward to seeing you in Dublin, next year.

Games Keep You Forever Young in Mind and Body

Lucia Pannese(✉)

imaginary srl, via Mauro Macchi 50, 20124 Milano, Italy
lucia.pannese@i-maginary.it

Abstract. In 2012, people aged 65 or above accounted for nearly one-fifth of the population of the European Union [1] and this figure is expected to reach 30 % by 2060 [2]. In other words, we are witnessing a demographic shift: the number of seniors who need support is growing whilst there is a decline in the percentage of the working population contributing to their support. This disproportion and the resulting tensions in the health and care system is one of the so-called "grand challenges [3]" that the EU is called to face. In this context, this speech will give an overview of several research approaches and studies, as well as design and development activities for games, including examples and lessons learned ranging from preventative healthcare in teen-agers through (home) rehabilitation and active ageing, to new emerging technology trends such as the oculus rift® and the omni virtuix®.

Keywords: Health games · Virtual reality · Rehabilitation · Active ageing

1 Introduction

The ageing society is a phenomenon created by a combination of factors which include improved living standards, better healthcare and efficient food manufacturing and distribution. The projected life expectancy in the developed world is steadily increasing but conditions related to old age such as dementia and mobility problems place an increased burden on welfare services. Even healthy elderly people in retirement create demands on society as their lifestyle is funded by pension schemes which are often based on shorter life expectancies.

The traditional sustainable society model in which a lifetime's work and contribution to society was rewarded by a golden retirement has been challenged by the problems of longer lifespans, falling birth rates and youth unemployment, all of which create a situation in which a smaller active workforce is effectively financing a growing population of retired people. Eurostat's projections by 2080 foresee the old-age dependency ratio to almost double from 28.1 % in 2014 to 51.0 %.

At the same time, today's society is shaped by technology in unprecedented ways. We all face disruptive changes in our lives and new challenges which, paradoxically, can be both created and addressed by the various digital technologies that inform, empower and influence individual citizens on a massive scale. There has been no previous period in history where millions of ordinary citizens have been able to freely access knowledge and simultaneously share their lives and opinions with a global audience. For these

C. Vaz de Carvalho et al. (Eds.): SGAMES 2015, LNICST 161, pp. 6–8, 2016.
DOI: 10.1007/978-3-319-29060-7_2

reasons, whilst the healthcare system is forced to face a huge reorganization and to find ways to reduce costs, including prevention programs that do not include active ageing (but that already start at a young age), we are also witnessing a shift in power, in which patients are increasingly directly managing their own health.

In this context, the speech describes how enabling technologies such as serious games and virtual reality, backed up with big data (e.g. coming from sensors) and other largely available technologies like analytics, have opened up a new opportunity space in the health market. But, in order to be considered an effective solution that can deliver the promised results in medical terms, and be engaging and usable by the target group for which it was developed, design has to follow specific rules and sound methodologies.

2 Serious Game Research

2.1 Physical and Cognitive Rehabilitation

Elderly people are a very special target group but, despite the fact that many people regard older people as scared or not inclined to use technology, the reality is that they are largely eager to experience virtual environments. Of course, games and digital solutions in general have to be designed to take their expectations and needs into serious consideration. Several solutions studied by imaginary in the course of many research projects will be presented, together with lessons learned whilst co-designing solutions with elderly people.

2.2 Active Ageing

Ideally, active ageing solutions should simultaneously take several aspects into consideration. This is what the EU project DOREMI [4] is doing by including cognitive and physical exercise together with socialization within the same gamified environment: thus every single exercise is a mini-game and all results are collected together in an integrated environment working with gamification mechanics.

2.3 Prevention in the Young Population

Whilst the ageing population is growing in number, the youth population is witnessing a progressive increase in phenomena which can result in severe pathologies (not necessarily only at an older age), such as obesity arising both from poor nutrition and sedentary lifestyles. Therefore, in order to fully address healthcare as a bigger picture, prevention programs have to be put in place targeting the youth population. This is what the EU project PEGASO [5] is dealing with, where a pervasive game is mixing actions in the real and virtual world to raise awareness in teens against obesity: whilst a bracelet is collecting inputs about physical movement, an energy bar is loaded in the virtual world. The serious game is then adapting to the available energy level: the more energy, the more fun the game.

References

1. http://ec.europa.eu/eurostat/statistics-explained/images/b/b7/Population_age_structure_by_major_age_groups%2C_2002_and_2012_%28%25_of_the_total_population%29_YB14.png
2. http://ec.europa.eu/economy_finance/articles/structural_reforms/2012-05-15_ageing_report_en.htm
3. Leijten, J., Butter, M., Kohl, J., Leis, M., Gehrt, D.: Study to assist the European Research Area Board: Investing in Research and Innovation for Grand Challenges (2012). http://ec.europa.eu/research/erab/pdf/erab-study-grand-challanages-2012_en.pdf
4. http://www.doremi-fp7.eu
5. http://www.pegasof4f.eu

How Fun Can a Serious Game Be?

Janet C. Read(✉)

Child Computer Interaction Group, University of Central Lancashire, Preston, UK
jcread@uclan.ac.uk

Abstract. This paper will explore how fun can be and might be designed into serious games for children. Three projects are described and then the tensions around designing for fun and education are unpicked with consideration of the roles of children in the design of these serious games.

Keywords: Serious games · Children · Fun · Learning

1 Introduction

The serious games industry has grown up around a premise that when learning is embodied within a game environment the learning experience is improved in some way when compared with more traditional instructional methods like the lecture (for example). When Clark Abt wrote his book on serious games in 1970, he talked about the elements that games brought; procedures, rules, participants, information, moves, winning and losing and he captured the key motivations for playing as being amusement, play, gain, competition, and opposition. [1] When referring to serious games he uses this to refer to the matter of the game – for example it being around a thing of great importance - as opposed to the attitude of the player. He writes 'games can be serious without being solemn, interesting without being hilarious, purposeful without being humourless'.

Research has shown that with the right balance, serious games can be used to instruct in very serious things. Many studies have suggested that the main addition to learning, brought by a serious game, is intrinsic motivation. Increased motivation has been shown, time and again, to have a positive impact on learning [2, 3]. That said, even after several decades of research, the jury is still out on the specific learning effects of serious games.

This tension, between a game that has to bring motivation and information while also allowing some humour and some amusement is particularly interesting when the intended players of the 'serious game' are children. Research has suggested that what is needed for improved learning and enhanced motivation is congruence and appeal. Congruence is the fit of the game narrative to the educational goals, and appeal is associated with the game mechanics and the right balance of challenge, fantasy, and curiosity [4].

C. Vaz de Carvalho et al. (Eds.): SGAMES 2015, LNICST 161, pp. 9–11, 2016.
DOI: 10.1007/978-3-319-29060-7_3

2 Three Projects

The UThink project was funded by the Esmee Fairburn foundation and aimed to develop a serious game to instruct teenagers in ways to regulate their emotional intelligence. There was a very serious aspect to this project as low emotional intelligence is correlated with teenagers getting into conflict situations with authority figures. This project took a set of already assembled worksheets, that had previously been used with teenagers in one on one sessions with caseworkers, and sought to embed the learning from those worksheets into a game. The novelty in the research project was the decision to work with a set of teenagers who were themselves already low in emotional intelligence and to have them co-design the game elements that would later be built into the game. The fun, therefore, in this serious game situation began at the point of design where teenagers used plasticine and biscuits as design props [5].

The UMSIC project was a cross European project that sought to create a music game to promote inclusion and cooperation between children. One of the target groups for this project was newly immigrant children who did not have the language of the country in which they were situated. This is clearly a very serious problem for European migrants and those migrating into Europe from several parts of Africa. These children, often with very little understanding of why, find themselves in schools that are unequipped to meet all their needs. Children contributing ideas for the design of 'inclusive games' were encouraged to design for Mr Hippo, who was a hippo who had happened to come into school that day. In creating a fun entry to the serious elements of the game - that Mr Hippo spoke no English, and that Mr Hippo had no fingers, children were able to empathise with the situation of the target players of the game and thus design into a space that they had hitherto not understood. In the context of this project, the design of the game elements was actually part of the solution as it became a process of education in itself for the children who volunteered ideas [6, 7].

Children designing for others has been a recent theme of our work in serious games design. The ChiCI in Africa project aimed to build a serious game to teach children the importance of careful hand washing in order to avoid water borne illnesses. There is little that is more serious, in terms of serious games, than a game that can, by clear instruction, save the lives of children. This game was to be shipped to rural Africa as part of a package of technology that included solar charging devices, tablet PCs and lighting. Designing this game involved a group of children in the UK having the problem explained to them before they then worked in small teams to sketch out the game story [8].

3 Where Is the Fun?

When considering fun in the context of serious games, there can be fun in the playing of the games, fun in the design of the games and fun in the understanding of the contexts. Where children are the recipients of the games then fun has to be a designed in component. The challenge is that if the game is too fun then maybe that fun might affect the learning – as it is the learning that is so important.

When children design serious games for other children, the discussion with the children has to stress the elements of learning. In the ChiCI for Africa project, the children doing the designs were focussed on the instructional, rather than the fun, elements of the game and consequently the designs were not so fun [9]. In the UThink project, the teenagers designing the games focussed very much on the fun aspects rather than on the learning and so the learning had to be layered into the fun aspects of the design and this did cause some design disparity [10]. When children designed for Mr Hippo they became engrossed in the needs of the players of the game to the extent that neither learning nor fun were all that evident in the game [6].

These three studies evidence a triangle of needs that require to be met in the design process where serious games are involved. The laying out of the design activity in order that these needs can be all conveyed is unpicked in the presentation.

Acknowledgments. Thanks to the ChiCI team members who have assisted in bringing these thoughts together.

References

1. Abt, C.C.: Serious Games. Viking Compass, New York (1975)
2. Batson, L., Feinberg, S.: Designs that enhance motivation and learning for teenagers. Electron. J. Integr. Technol. Educ. **5**, 34–43 (2006)
3. Malone, T.W., Lepper, M.R.: Making learning fun: a taxonomy of intrinsic motivations for learning. In: Snow, R.E., Farr, M.J. (eds.) Aptitude, Learning and Instruction. Cognitive and Affective Process Analysis, vol. 5, pp. 223–253. Erlbaum, Hillsdale (1987)
4. Charsky, D., Ressler, W.: Games are made for fun: lessons on the effects of concept maps in the classroom use of computer games. Comput. Educ. **56**(3), 604–615 (2011)
5. Mazzone, E., Read, J.C., Beale, R.: Design with and for disaffected teenagers. In: Nordichi 2008. ACM Press, Lund (2008)
6. Read, J.C., et al.: Designing for Mr Hippo – introducing concepts of marginalisation to children designers. In: Workshop on Designing for Marginalized Children, IDC 2009. ACM, Italy (2009)
7. Heikkinen, K., et al.: Designing mobile applications for children. User Requirements Wireless **42**, 7 (2015)
8. Sim, G., et al.: From England to Uganda: Children Designing and Evaluating Serious Games. Hum.-Comput. Interact. **30**(3–4), 263–293 (2014)
9. Read, J.C., et al.: Children Designing Serious Games. EAI Trans. Serious Games **13**(1), 5 (2013)
10. Mazzone, E., Read, J.C., Beale, R.: Understanding children's contributions during informant design. In: BCS-HCI 2008. BCS (2008)

Applying a Serious Game Quality Model

Lilia García-Mundo(✉), Marcela Genero, and Mario Piattini

Institute of Technologies and Informations Systems,
University of Castilla-La Mancha,
Paseo de la Universidad, 4, 13071 Ciudad Real, Spain
liliacarmen.garcia@alu.uclm.es,
{marcela.genero,mario.piattini}@uclm.es

Abstract. This paper has the following goals: (1) To introduce a preliminary version of a Serious Game Quality Model (QSGame-Model), (2) To present an example of the application of this model and (3) To outline the future empirical studies that we plan to perform in order to refine and validate the model.

Keywords: QSGame-Model · Quality model · Serious Game · Survey · Experiment

1 Introduction

A Serious Game (SG) is a game whose main purpose goes beyond than mere entertainment [1]. Although these games are widely used in education, they can also be applied to areas as varied as defense, scientific exploration, health care, emergency management, city planning, engineering, religion, and politics. SGs are a rapidly-emerging area of opportunity, as well as being a growing market [2] and can be a means of achieving important objectives from both personal and institutional points of view; all these aspects make them vitally important. The social impact of SGs is very high, due to the fact that the number of SGs users is growing day-by-day. We thus believe that the quality of SGs is a high priority, and consider it is our duty as researchers and practitioners to ensure this quality. That concern led us to establish our research objective, which was to propose and validate a quality model adapted specifically to SGs. We started by carrying out a systematic mapping study (SMS), aiming to discover the current state-of-the-art on research into SG Quality [3]. This literature review manifested that researchers are concerned about SG quality, but there is no consensus on what the most relevant quality characteristics SGs are desired to fulfill. For that reason we have proposed a preliminary version of a product quality model for SGs, called QSGame-Model [4], a version which is based mainly on the current standard on software product quality, the ISO/IEC 25010 [5]. In [4], we presented the complete process of the construction of the QSGame-Model, but we did not give any example of its application. The main goal of this paper is to illustrate the use of the QSGame-Model for evaluating a SG. This application example will very useful for professionals in software quality and in SGs development, giving an illustration that makes the quality model easier to understand. The remainder of this document is organized as follows. Section 2 gives a brief introduction to the QSGame-Model.

C. Vaz de Carvalho et al. (Eds.): SGAMES 2015, LNICST 161, pp. 12–20, 2016.
DOI: 10.1007/978-3-319-29060-7_4

Section 3 describes an example of how to evaluate the quality of SGs using the QSGame-Model, and Sect. 4 presents general ideas for the future empirical studies we are planning to perform in order to refine and validate the model. Finally, our main conclusions and ideas for future work will be set out in Sect. 5.

2 The QSGame-Model

The QSGame-Model presented in [4] was based on the generic ISO/IEC 25010 [5] standard and was adapted to the SG domain. This standard establishes high-level quality concepts, which must be adapted or extended if they are to be useful in specific domains. We decided to adapt our model using the top-down methodology proposed by Franch and Carvallo [6]. The detailed steps followed to define QSGame-Model can be found in [4].

Results of the state-of-the-art on SG quality [3] showed us the elements addressed by research in this field. Based on these results, we considered the incorporation of specific SG attributes applied to SG which are not defined in the standard product quality model [5].

We incorporated different attributes to the Functional Suitability sub-characteristics: Functional completeness, Functional correctness and Functional appropriateness; and to the Usability sub-characteristics: Appropriateness recognizability, Learnability, Operability, User interface aesthetics, and Accessibility. The incorporation of attributes in these two characteristics came about because we believe they are directly associated with the elements that facilitate the flow experience [7] (objectives and clear rules, feedback, balance between challenges and skills and concentration). In addition, these two characteristics were those addressed most by research according to the SMS on SG quality [3] findings. By way of example, Fig. 1 shows the sub-characteristics and attributes of Functional Suitability, while the measures for each attribute are presented in the following section. The complete description of the QSGame-Model can be accessed at http://alarcos.esi.uclm.es/SeriousGamesProductQualityModel/.

3 Applying the QSGame-Model

In this section we will present an example of the evaluation of the Functional Suitability characteristic of a prototype of an SG, called "Ceebot-A demo 1.17" [8]. The Functional Suitability characteristic is defined as the *Degree to which an SG provides functions that meet stated and implied needs when used under specified conditions.* Ceebot is an SG (Fig. 1) whose main objective is for users to learn Programming while having fun. Ceeboot-A demo requires the player to cover two main topics (Fundamentals and Continuation) by carrying out the functions shown in Table 1. For each of the functions, the game provides all the instructions needed for completion.

We will now go on to describe each of the measures that have been proposed to evaluate each of the attributes of the Functional Suitability sub-characteristics,

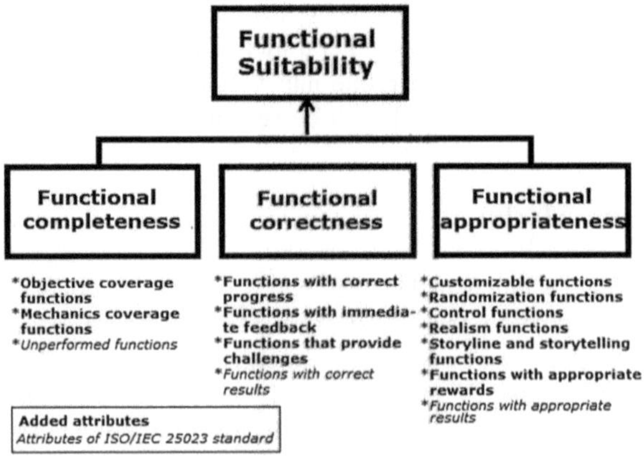

Fig. 1. Functional suitability: sub-characteristics and attributes

Table 1. CBoot-A functions.

Function name	Function objective
1. Move	Just move forwards
2. The straight line	Draw a perfect straight line
3. First turn	Draw a large "L"
4. Massacre 1	Destroy three targets with a short program
5. Massacre 2	Use a loop to blow up six targets

providing results of their evaluation (see Tables 2, 3 and 4). Each measure includes the measure name, measure description, measurement function, the value obtained and the comments that are needed to clarify some aspect of the values obtained.

The Functional Completeness sub-characteristic is defined as the *Degree to which the set of SG functions covers all the specified tasks and user objectives.*

The Functional Correctness sub-characteristic is defined as the Degree *to which an SG provides the correct results with the needed degree of precision.*

Functional Appropriateness sub-characteristic is defined as *Degree to which the SG functions facilitate the accomplishment of specified SG tasks and objectives.*

The results obtained from the evaluation of all the quality attributes of the Functional Suitability characteristic revealed that Ceebot-A is of good quality with respect to this characteristic, except for the following measures (Fig. 2):

- Mechanics coverage: The value obtained in the evaluation was 0.6, because 2 of the functions do not provide rewards when the player achieves the function objective (Table 2). To improve this result to its maximum value of 1, these two functions should provide rewards when the player achieves the goal.
- Functional Randomization and Functional Control: The value of 0 obtained in those measures shows that none of the functions has actions or tasks that occur in random order, and that the game does not allow the user to choose different controls for operating the game (Table 3). These results could be improved to reach the value of

Table 2. Functional completeness sub-characteristic.

Measure name	Measure description	Measurement function	Measure value/Comment
Objective coverage	How complete is the implementation according to established objectives in requirement specifications?	X = 1 − A / B A = number of functions missing B = number of total functions specified X [0,1]; the closer to 1 the better A missing function is detected when the SG does not have the ability to perform a function related to an established objective on requirements.	A = 0; B = 5 X = 1 − 0 / 5 = **1** Although requirement specification is needed to evaluate this measurement, in this evaluation example we are assuming all objectives established were implemented.
Mechanics coverage	How complete is the implementation of game mechanics in SG functions so that each function objective established provides a challenge, and each challenge is expected to offer a reward?	X = 1 − A / B A = number of functions missing B = number of total functions specified X [0,1]; the closer to 1 the better A missing function is detected when the SG does not have the ability to perform a function with mechanics.	A = 2; B = 5 X = 1− 2 / 5 = **0,6** Functions "Move" (1) and "The straight line" (2) do not provide rewards (2 of 5).

1 if, in the first case, the 5 functions had tasks that occur in random order, or if, in the second case, the game allowed the user to choose different controls to operate it.

- Appropriateness Rewards: The value of 0.4 obtained shows that just 2 of the 5 functions offer appropriate rewards (Table 3). This value could be improved to reach a value of 1 if the 5 functions provided appropriate rewards.

4 Outline of the Future Refinement and Validation of the QSGame-Model

Our future work will focus mainly on the refinement and validation of QSGame-Model. To do this, we have first constructed a survey that we plan to distribute to the largest possible number of experts in SG development and teaching, to ask them about the relevance and understandability of each of the quality attributes defined in the QSGame-Model. Table 5 shows an example of a question on the survey; it corresponds to Objective Coverage Function, an attribute of the Functional completeness sub-characteristic. To contextualize the survey responses, we have included a block of

Table 3. Functional correctness sub-characteristic.

Measure name	Measure description	Measurement function	Measure value/Comment
Functional progress	To what extent do functions provide a correct and accurate score in order to signal the player's progress or advancement in the game?	X = A / B A = number of functions which provide correct and accurate score to signal progress B = number of total functions of SG X [0,1]; the closer to 1 the better	A = 5; B = 5 X = 5 / 5 = **1** 5 out of 5 functions provide correct progress.
Functional immediate feedback	To what extent do functions provide the player with immediate feedback in response to incorrect action?	X = A / B A = number of functions which offer immediate feedback to the player in response to incorrect action B = number of total functions of SG X [0,1]; the closer to 1 the better	A = 5; B = 5 X = 5 / 5 = **1** 5 out of 5 functions offer immediate feedback to the player in response to incorrect action.
Functional challenge provided	To what extent do functions allow the SG user to set levels of difficulty in challenges that adapt to their particular skills?	X = A / B A = number of functions allow the SG user to set levels of difficulty in challenges that adapt their skills B = number of total functions of SG X [0,1]; the closer to 1 the better	A = 5; B = 5 X = 5 / 5 = **1** Although the CeeBot-A demo version does not allow the reuse of the option of establishing levels of difficulty in challenges, we are assuming this would be possible; the game has the option of setting those levels.

questions regarding demographic information about the respondents, such as their gender, education level, country in which they work, experience in video game and SG development, etc.

Once the QSGame-Model has been refined, we will conduct experiments to obtain empirical evidence on its usefulness, i.e., to obtain empirical evidence that will allow us to ascertain whether the presence of the model allows SG developers to build better quality SGs. We will therefore have obtained a quality model for SG that has been agreed on by experts and which is also useful for SG developers.

Table 4. Functional appropriateness sub-characteristic.

Measure name	Measure description	Measurement function	Measure value/Comment
Functional customization	Does the SG allow the user to establish particular preferences, e.g. to be identified as a character of a particular sex or given appearance, etc.?	X = yes or not If the game allows the user to establish particular preferences, X value will be "1"; otherwise X value will be "0" X [0 or 1]; 1 is better	X = **1**
Functional randomization	What proportion of the implemented functions has actions or tasks produced in random order?	X = A / B A = number of implemented functions which have actions or tasks produced in random order B = number of total functions of SG X [0,1]; the closer to 1 the better	A = 0; B = 5 X = 0 / 5 = **0** 0 out of 5 implemented functions have actions or tasks produced in random order.
Functional control	Do the game functions allow the user to choose different controls for operating the game?	X = yes or no If the game allows the user to choose different controls for operating the game, X value will be "1", otherwise X value will be "0" X [0 or 1]; 1 is better	X = **0**
Functional realism	What amount of the implemented functions allows that virtual world to be as close as possible to the real world?	X = A / B A = number of implemented functions which allows the virtual world to be as close as possible to the real world. B = number of total functions of SG X [0,1]; the closer to 1 the better	A = 5; B = 5 X = 5 / 5 = **1** 5 out of 5 implemented functions allow the virtual world to be as close as possible to the real world.
Functional storyline and storytelling	What amount of the implemented functions has tasks	X = A / B A = number of implemented	A = 5; B = 5 X = 5 / 5 = 1

(*Continued*)

Table 4. (*Continued*)

Measure name	Measure description	Measurement function	Measure value/Comment
	and activities relevant to the storyline and storytelling being conducted throughout the game?	functions which has tasks and activities relevant to the storyline and storytelling B = number of total functions of SG X [0,1]; the closer to 1 the better	5 out of 5 implemented functions have tasks and activities relevant to the storyline and storytelling.
Appropriateness of reward	What proportion of the implemented functions offered appropriate rewards, in relation to the challenge achieved?	X = A / B A = number of the implemented functions which offer appropriate rewards B = number of total functions of SG X [0,1]; the closer to 1 the better	A = 2; B = 5 X = 2 / 5 = **0,4** Function "Massacre 1" (4) and "Massacre 2" (5) provide appropriate rewards (2 of 5).

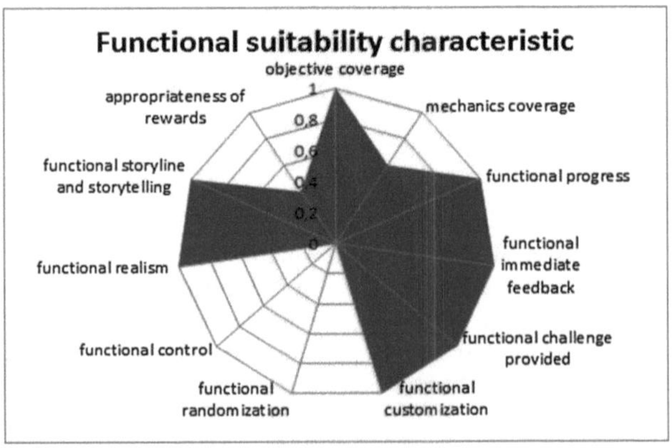

Fig. 2. Functional suitability characteristic: evaluation results.

Table 5. Example question on the survey of objective coverage function on functional completeness sub-characteristic.

Num	Question description		
1.	The Serious Game should have all the functions that are necessary to attain the objectives established in the requirements specification.		
	¿Do you understand this definition clearly? **Yes No**		
	¿How important do you consider the quality attribute that has been defined?		
	It is not important	**It is quite important**	**It is very important**
	Observations:		

5 Conclusions and Future Work

The main contribution of this paper is to present an example of the application of a product quality model specifically for SGs (QSGame-Model), which we proposed in [4]. We have in particular evaluated the Functional Suitability of an SG for learning Programming, called SG Ceebot-A [8] and we have also provided some suggestions for the improvement of the game. In addition, we have outlined the refinement and validation activities we are planning to perform in the near future. Our final goal is to obtain an SG quality model that has been agreed on by experts and which will be useful in practice, thus contributing to the building of higher quality SGs by SG developers.

Acknowledgments. This work has been funded by the following projects: GEODAS-BC (Ministerio de Economía y Competitividad and Fondo Europeo de Desarrollo Regional FEDER, TIN2012-37493-C03-01) and IMPACTUM (Consejería de Educación, Ciencia y Cultura de la Junta de Comunidades de Castilla La Mancha, y Fondo Europeo de Desarrollo Regional FEDER, PEII11-0330-4414). We would also like to thank the "Instituto Tecnológico de Ciudad Victoria" and PRODEP for granting the first author the scholarship that made it possible to complete the research work presented in this paper.

References

1. Susi, T., Johannesson, M., Backlund, P.: Serious Games – An Overview. Technical report, School of Humanities and Informatics University of Skövde Sweden (2007)
2. Michael, D.R., Chen, S.L.: Serious Games: Games that Educate, Train and Inform. Muska and Lipman/Premier-Trade (2005)
3. Vargas, J., Garcia-Mundo, L., Genero, M., Piattini, M.: A systematic mapping study on serious game quality. In: 18th International Conference on Evaluation and Assessment in Software Engineering (EASE 2014), vol. 15. ACM, New York (2014)
4. García-Mundo, L., Genero, M., Piattini, M.: Towards a construction and validation of a serious game product quality model. In: 7th International Conference on Games and Virtual Worlds for Serious Applications (VS-Games 2015), pp. 1–8. IEEE (2015)

5. ISO/IEC: ISO/IEC IS 25010: Systems and Software Engineering - Systems and Software Quality Requirements and Evaluation (SQuaRE) - System and Software Quality Models, ISO (International Organization for Standarization) (2011)
6. Franch, X., Carvallo, J.P.: Using quality models in software package selection. IEEE Softw. **20**(1), 34–41 (2003)
7. Csikszentmihalyi, M.: Flow: The Psychology of Optimal Experience. Harper Perennial, New York (1991)
8. EPSITEC games, http://www.ceebot.com/ceebot/family-e.php

Dynamic Serious Games Balancing

Carlos Vaz de Carvalho(✉)

GILT-ISEP, Rua Dr. António Bernardino de Almeida, 431, 4200-072 Porto, Portugal
cmc@isep.ipp.pt

Abstract. The user's interest in a game is difficult to be raised and even more difficult to be maintained. The game must be addictive and correspond to the users' interest to make sure he/she doesn't feel attracted to other competing games. Therefore specific, user-adapted mechanisms are necessary to keep their interest and motivation. Dynamic game balancing (DGB) is the process of changing game parameters in real-time, according to the users' detected ability, in order to provide him/her with a tight fit challenge (neither too easy nor too difficult). A user model must be created for each player, based on data collected before and during game play focusing on interaction statistics and eventually on physiological signals. The use of identical mechanisms adjusted to the objectives of Serious Games implies changes to the design of the DGB methodology. This article presents the main theoretical aspects of this process.

Keywords: Serious Games · Dynamic game balancing

1 Introduction

Games involve mental and physical stimulation and force the player to decide, to choose, to define priorities, to solve problems, etc. Games can also be social environments, sometimes involving large distributed communities where social skills are paramount. They imply self-learning abilities (players are often required to seek out information to master the game itself), allow transfer of learning from other realities and are inherently experiential with the engagement of multiple senses. Therefore, game environments are excellent tools because they can replicate real contexts or even provide situations that occur in very specific circumstances while retaining the players' motivation.

But the user's interest is difficult to be raised and even more difficult to be maintained. Therefore specific, user-adapted mechanisms are necessary to keep their interest and motivation. Dynamic game balancing (DGB) is the process of changing game parameters in real-time, according to the users' detected ability, in order to provide them with a tight-fit challenge (neither too easy nor too difficult). A user model is individually created for each player, based on data collected before and during game play focusing on interaction statistics and eventually on physiological signals. Typical collected data (or game play metrics) can be object interaction, object trade, navigation in the environment, average playtime, damage dealt per session, etc.

C. Vaz de Carvalho et al. (Eds.): SGAMES 2015, LNICST 161, pp. 21–27, 2016.
DOI: 10.1007/978-3-319-29060-7_5

Game play metrics can be subdivided into the following three categories:

- In-game: Covers all in-game actions and behaviors of players, including navigation and interaction with game assets such as objects and entities.
- Interface: Assesses all the player interactions with the game interface and menus, like setting game variables.
- System: Covers the game actions initiated to respond to player actions.

Serious Games are games that do not have entertainment as the main objective and are used to develop skills and competences related to education, government, corporate training, health and others. In fact, the main emphasis of serious games is still the educational domain with focus on learning and training and the application of new pedagogies. Nevertheless Serious Games are still games insofar they provide an entertainment-oriented, rule-based context, with clear goals. Therefore the use of DGB is still very important to keep the user motivated but should be extended to include a dimension that relates to the "serious" goals of the game which requires the collection of specific game analytics data concerned with those objectives.

This article envisages the definition, implementation and validation of a DGB methodology specially designed for Serious Games where the entertainment aspect is considered in equal terms with the serious objectives of the game, which requires special game analytics techniques. In terms of validation two different areas of application will be covered: on one side, educational games (for its importance in terms of the existing market) and, on the other side, exergames, that is games that motivate the user to have a healthier lifestyle by engaging them in physical activities.

Therefore, in the end it will be possible to obtain a methodological approach to this issue based on a set of methods for game analytics, player modeling and dynamic game balancing, instantiated for two specific areas of application: education and physical fitness. The tools developed for these two areas will be easily adaptable for other purposes in the same area (for instance, for different levels of education or professional/amateur physical fitness).

2 State of the Art

A game is a goal directed and competitive activity conducted within a framework of agreed rules [1]. Or "A game is a system in which players engage in an artificial conflict, defined by rules, that results in a quantifiable outcome" [2]. The rules establish what a player can or cannot do, and what the behavioral consequences of actions may be within the world of the game. The game offers a structured and oriented context (meaning) to play which is a voluntary activity, intrinsically motivated, enjoyable and for recreation, in a non real context, requiring active participation. Overmars stated that "Playing a Game is about making Decisions, taking Control and reaching Goals" [3]. Prensky identified the following characteristics of games [4]:

- Games are a form of fun. That gives us enjoyment and pleasure.
- Games are a form of play. That gives us intense and passionate involvement.
- Games have rules. That gives us structure.

- Games have goals. That gives us motivation.
- Games are interactive. That gives us doing.
- Games are adaptive. That gives us flow.
- Games have outcomes and feedback. That gives us learning.
- Games have win states. That gives us ego gratification.
- Games have conflict/competition/challenge/opposition. That gives us ad adrenaline.
- Games have problem solving. That sparks our creativity.
- Games have interaction. That gives us social groups.
- Games have representation and story. That gives us emotion.

Games can be instantiated for serious purposes as they involve mental and physical stimulation and they allow developing practical skills – they force the player to decide, to choose, to define priorities, to solve problems, etc. When games involve social environments, sometimes involving large distributed communities, they support the development of social competencies. Games develop the users' self learning abilities (players are often required to seek out information to master the game itself), they allow transfer of learning from other realities and are inherently experiential with the engagement of multiple senses.

Serious Games (SG) are games that do not have entertainment as the main objective. They are a "a mental contest, played with a computer in accordance with specific rules, that uses entertainment to further government or corporate training, education, health, public policy, and strategic communication objectives" [5]. Serious games "are games insofar as they have rules, simulate behaviors, accept input from the player, and provide feedback within the context of the rules and behaviors" [6]. So, even if the main objective of a SG is not entertainment, it must provide the user with a context that engages and motivates him/her. Or, in the words of Csikszentmihalyi, the user should be in flow: "People are happiest when they are in a state of flow— a state of concentration or complete absorption with the activity at hand and the situation. It is a state in which people are so involved in an activity that nothing else seems to matter" [7].

Dynamic Game Balancing (DGB) is the process of real-time adjustment of game parameters so that the faced challenges and environment fit the player's ability, therefore keeping the player in *Flow*. This way the player will not be bored (if the game is too easy) or anxious (if it is too hard) and will remain motivated to play the game. DGB provides an individualized approach to a game and replaces the standard approach, common for all the players, despite their previous gaming experience, through an increasing linear difficulty approach or through a difficulty ladder (levels). DGB requires the definition of a Player Model, constructed by the collection of pregame and real-time game data. Andrade et al. present two dimensions of DGB: competence vs. performance that is the understanding and mastering of the game vs the capacity to efficiently tackle with its challenges [8].

Game analytics (GA), the set of methods designed to collect and interpret that data, are mostly related to game play metrics, that is information about the actual behavior of the user as a player inside the game: object interaction, object trade, navigation in the environment, actions and position of the player's character, results in each level, time spent, interactions with the game interface and menus, etc.

For Serious Games, DGB must include a component related to the serious objectives of the game. The entertainment aspect of the game cannot hide the skill or competence development objective (SCDO) and therefore must be tuned to include this concern. Game analytics should, at the same time, provide data that allows to assess how the player is progressing towards those serious goals.

DGB for Serious Games is a novel area without major research published unlike DGB for "normal" games where a few approaches have been used: [8] presented an approach where agents were trained to play against the human player at his/her skill level; in [9] genetic algorithms techniques the agents that best fit the user level; In [10], artificial neural networks (ANN) and fuzzy neural networks are used to estimate the parameters that provide engaging game play. None of these approaches has been extensively validated so research work is required to determine the best process to collect game analytics data and to use it for DGB but also to analyze the progress towards a DSGB Dynamic Serious Game Balancing.

Further research is also required to establish a taxonomic approach to Serious Games that delimits the DSGB methods and parameters adequate to each area of application. It is clear that serious games with educational purposes are quite different from serious games for marketing purposes, for instance. But, although it is possible to create a methodology that addresses the use of DSGB for serious games in general and develop a set of methods, data collection and analysis methods and technologies may not be, to a great extent, common. Therefore finding these specificities is a state of the art research.

3 Methods

The objectives of the project described in this article are:

- To design a methodology and corresponding methods for DSGB;
- To implement and validate the methodology with two case studies: one for educational purposes and another for fitness (personal health) purposes. Basically, two serious games will be developed, one for each area, with DSGB support.

The validation methodology is quite complex: on one side it will be necessary to evaluate the actual results of the use of the two serious games and on the other it will be necessary to assess the actual adequacy of the methodology, methods and tools. Typically Serious Games are assessed in the multiple domains of usability, game play and content (as the serious objective). Therefore the data collected must answer very different questions like:

- Is the game easy to learn and to play?
- Is the user interface (controls and navigation) adequate?
- Are the game play elements adequate to the target group.
- Is the game entertaining for them?
- Do the player decisions have a crucial role in the game result?
- Are the contents embedded in the game adequate to achieve the expected development of knowledge, skill, competence, awareness…?
- Did the player learned/developed what was intended?

- Did the player receive the message that was planned to transmit?
- Did the player changed convictions/opinions after playing the game?

The DSGB methodology, although roughly following existing DGB approaches, is still innovative and new. Therefore, the complexity of this goal requires that strong and careful steps for analysis, design, development, validation and testing are in place. This methodology is concreted in the following set of tasks:

- Project Management and Quality Assurance: Integrates project planning and monitoring to ensure a full quality assurance approach. This task deals with project planning, monitoring and quality assurance and it will be led by the IR. This task will also deal with the process of quality assurance of the project methodology and results of the project. It will be accomplished through a continuous process of monitoring, internal and external evaluation and methodology, methods and tools validation. Therefore it will have a component of formative evaluation (during the project) and summative evaluation (at the end) of the Project, and will focus on Activities and Products. The methodology adopted includes the analysis of quantitative and qualitative data, focusing as much on processes / methodologies as products / results.
- Specification and Analysis: This task will handle the identification of the state of the art in the multiple domains addressed by the project and the specification of the methodology. This task will produce a set of publishable deliverables like a survey on DGB methods and tools, a survey on game analytics, a survey on game development tools and an article about the definition of the Player Model (PM). This task will also handle the identification of the state of the art in the multiple domains addressed by the project and the specification of the methodology. This task will produce a set of publishable deliverables like a survey on DGB methods and tools, a survey on game analytics, a survey on game development tools and an article about the definition of the Player Model (PM). Therefore it includes the conceptual aspects but also the technical aspects related to the tools. The design and specification will be lead by the PhD researchers experts in their specific areas. External consultants will be involved to provide their expertise.
- Design of the DSGB methodology: This task relates to the design of the SGDBG methodology, methods and tools. It will also include the complete design of the two case studies: one for educational purposes and another for personal fitness purposes. This task is highly dependent on the results of the previous task where a comparison between the different available technologies will lead to a decision.
- Development of the serious games: This task integrates the activities related to the actual development of the games and tools (including data collection tools). A Rapid Prototyping Approach will be preferred (which implies a regular involvement of the users).
- Validation and Test: This task corresponds to the implementation of the validation phase. It will start by identifying the users that will be involved in the implementation. The second task is to make a detailed plan. The next task is to actually implement all the activities, according to the project plan. All of these processes will be evaluated continuously, so that results can contribute to an upgrade of the environment, the contents and the pedagogical methodology itself.

4 Conclusions

Serious games are games that do not have entertainment as the main objective. Nevertheless they are games, so they must keep the user motivated and interested, in "flow". Dynamic Games Balancing tries to adjust the difficulty levels of the challenges to the abilities of the player providing a tight fit match that prevents him/her from getting bored (when challenges are too easy) or anxious (when challenges are too difficult). For Serious Games, DGB must incorporate a new dimension related to the "serious" objectives of the game.

Dynamic Serious Games Balancing is therefore a new approach that tries to balance the challenges not only to the game play performance but also to the serious objective performance (have learning outcomes been achieved in educational games? has the advertising message caused an impact in advergames?). A Serious Player Model (SPM) based on the User Model of Adaptive Hypermedia Systems will be created incorporating all the relevant parameters of use. "Player modeling is, primarily, the study and use of artificial and computational intelligence (AI and CI) techniques for the construction of computational models of player behavior, cognition and emotion, as well as other aspects beyond their interaction with a game (such as their personality and cultural background)." [11]. The SPM extends this model into the player characteristics adequate for the serious game purpose. For instance, for an exergame the player model should incorporate physical parameters of the user, for educational games the SPM has to include parameters related to the knowledge, skills and competences pre and post serious game usage. The SPM integrates with the idea of Procedural Content Generation (PCG) that is the possibility of realtime generation of the game challenges based on a set of parameters instead of a complete, predetermined and fixed progress route. A simple example is Temple Run, a game where the player's route is always different based on instant random selection of a path and challenges from a predetermined set of paths and challenges.

Using DSGB, based on SPM, combining with PCG it is expected to create highly motivating, adaptive and personalized skill and competence development environments (but still games) that keep users involved for a long time therefore ensuring that they are focused on the "serious" objective. This approach implies the definition of methods to collect user data (game play, interaction and content) also known as game analytics. As serious games can have quite different purposes (educational, advertising, health, awareness raising) the actual tools to implement the methods must be different and the collected data also highly depends on the actual serious game objectives.

Acknowledgments. This work has been partly supported by the European Commission through its European Agency for Culture, Education, Audiovisual in the scope of the Lifelong Learning Programme, KA3 sub-programme, eCity project (ref. 543573-LLP-1-2013-1-PT-KA3-KA3MP).

References

1. Lindley, C.A.: Game Taxonomies: A High Level Framework for Game Analysis and Design (2003). Gamasutra.com
2. Salen, K., Zimmerman, E.: Rules of Play: Game Design Fundamentals. MIT Press, Cambridge (2003)

3. Overmars, M.: Game Maker Tutorial: Designing Good Games. YoYo Games Ltd., Dundee (2007)
4. Prensky, M.: Digital Game Based Learning. McGrawHill, New York (2001)
5. Zyda, M.: From visual simulation to virtual reality to games. IEEE Comput. **38**(9), 25–32 (2005). IEEE Computer Society
6. Michael, D., Chen, S.: Serious Games: Games that educate, train and inform (1ª ed.). Thomson (2006)
7. Csikszentmihalyi, M.: Beyond Boredom and Anxiety: Experiencing Flow in Work and Play. Jossey Bass, San Francisco (1975). ISBN 0875892612
8. Andrade, G., Ramalho, G., Santana, H., Corruble, V.: Challenge sensitive action selection: an application to game balancing. In: Proceedings of the IEEE/WIC/ACM International Conference on Intelligent Agent Technology (IAT 2005), Compiègne, France, pp. 194–200. IEEE Computer Society (2005)
9. Demasi, P., Cruz, A.: Online coevolution for action games. In: Proceedings of the 3rd International Conference on Intelligent Games and Simulation, London, pp. 113–120 (2002)
10. Yannakakis, G.M., Hallam, J.: Evolving opponents for interesting interactive computer games. In: Proceedings of the 8th International Conference on the Simulation of Adaptive Behavior (SAB 2004). From Animals to Animats 8, Los Angeles, California, United States, pp. 499–508. The MIT Press (2004)
11. Yannakakis, G., Spronck, P., Loiacono, D., Andre, E.: Player Modelling, Dagstuhl Publishing, Schloss Dagstuhl – LeibnizZentrum für Informatik, Germany (2013)

Relation Between Game Genres and Competences for In-Game Certification

Ricardo Baptista[1(✉)], António Coelho[1], and Carlos Vaz de Carvalho[2]

[1] DEI/FEUP - Faculty of Engineering, INESC TEC - INESC Technology and Science, University of Porto, Rua Dr. Roberto Frias no. 378, 4200-465 Porto, Portugal
rjvb@inesctec.pt, acoelho@fe.up.pt
[2] ISEP- Instituto Superior de Engenharia do Porto, Rua Dr. António Bernardino de Almeida, 431, 4200-072 Porto, Portugal
cvc@ipp.isep.pt

Abstract. Digital Games can be effective as learning tools, in applications that can be designated as Serious Games (SG), Games for Learning (GL) or Games-based learning (GBL). SG provide challenges in accordance with the intended learning objectives and can adapt and/or repeat (by allowing error recovering) them according to the learner's level. In training, this aspect is decisive in the acquisition of knowledge, experience and professional skills. The effectiveness of games-based training is directly related to the success on how the challenges promote the acquisition of skills, for which there is no optimal design methodology. This paper presents how a study that identifies the most appropriate game genres to develop specific skills and competences can be used to provide initial solutions to serious games design methodologies. The Triadic Certification model combines the competences defined for each training plan with the challenges designed for the serious games on a matrix that matches the needs and levels.

Keywords: Serious games · Skills · Competences · Assessment · Game genre · Game-based learning · Training certification

1 Introduction

The growing reputation of SG confirms its high value in education as well as the potential benefits of using video games to engage learners and to improve the learning effectiveness. Our aim in this paper is precisely to give a contribution to create initial solutions that identify with the most appropriate serious game genres and the game design guidelines to promote the successful training and certification of specific skills. With the In-Game Certification methodology approach we intend to define, verify and validate the game design contributions and how systems are capable to provide real learning experiences. The success of this proof of concept is defined by the player performance results into different training plans.

The methodology of this study includes three main references: a taxonomy of game genres (Action, Strategy, Role-Playing, Sports, Management Simulation, Adventure, Puzzle and Quiz) and its relation with standard competences and skills; the referential

C. Vaz de Carvalho et al. (Eds.): SGAMES 2015, LNICST 161, pp. 28–35, 2016.
DOI: 10.1007/978-3-319-29060-7_6

competence model as "a collection of competencies associated with the necessary attributes, behaviour, areas of knowledge, skills and abilities for a successful job performance" [1], called Educational Competency Wheel; and a certification model with the following axes: the identified skills (competences), mechanics based in game genres and training levels [20].

This paper is structured as follows: After this brief introduction, a section on the use of serious games for training and certification and game genres is presented. Section 3 describes the study on the relation between game genres and competences and Sect. 4 presents the integration of the results of this study with the in-game certification methodology. Finally, Sect. 5 presents conclusions and future work.

2 Serious Games for Training

Serious Games are becoming increasingly more popular in the corporate level as well as in research communities. SG are defined as games that aim to take advantage of all the features that make them fun and engaging [10], promoting the interest of trainees by making the educational subject and learning process exciting [2].

The research of Freitas and Jarvis [3] about Game-based Learning "shows some initial evidence of accelerating learning, increasing motivation and supporting the development of higher order cognitive thinking skills". The association of that with digital games, digital games–based learning, supports a new approach to learning because the player, which in the educational context is a learner, uses games to explore, discover, question and ultimately construct concepts and relationships in authentic contexts [4]. This study also concluded that games helped learners to understand very complex concepts more easily and also increased their motivation through a positive association between the learner and his learning. In this work it was also concluded that "the advantage of serious games approaches lies in their ability to create dedicated content for learning purposes, rather than to adapt existing leisure games to educational practices". These games are intentionally designed to help in learning, skills acquisition and behaviour change [5, 6]. The game design process becomes the key to achieve the learning outcomes through the game play.

A new contribution to skill training certification can be done by the Methodology for In-Game Certification [7] where several game design guidelines will be incorporated into a serious game to measure the training performance. This approach is composed by four steps which will be explain in Sect. 4 of this paper, and works as a communication support in favour of the dialectic between the trainer(s) and the game designer(s).

2.1 Training and Educational Competencies Standard

A competency is the capacity to apply or use a set of related knowledge, skills and abilities required to successfully perform a desired task. Lominger's set of sixty-seven competencies [8] became a universal common denominator as most of these competencies lead to task success.

This assessment tool is called Leadership Architect Competences and allows composing a list, using one or combining a few of the existing competency models, which encapsulates the competencies needed to succeed [1]. This competency model represents "a collection of competencies associated with a successful performance" [9]. In order to apply to education or training the same authors created together with Microsoft a similar approach called Education Competencies or Educational Competency Wheel [10]. This tool represents many of the necessary attributes, behaviour, areas of knowledge, skills and abilities for a successful job performance.

The table of competences, as seen in Table 1 consists of six core skill-sets and personality characteristics such as Individual Excellence, Organizational Skills, Courage, Results, Strategic Skills, and Operating Skills. These categories contain 44 competencies of Lominger's standard, but can be extended to other areas outside of education or training. The competency wheel provides other resources to help identify the core competencies, which are the ones associated with the success of an organization [9]. These resources include a definition, four levels of proficiency, sample interview questions, activities and resources for developing skills in order to help an organization achieve success.

Table 1. Educational Competency Wheel

Education Success Factors					
Individual excellence	**Organizational skills**	**Courage**	**Results**	**Strategic skills**	**Operating skills**
- Building effective teams (IE1) - Compassion (IE2) - Customer focus (IE3) - Humor (IE4) - Integrity and trust (IE5) - Interpersonal skills (IE6) - Listening (IE7) - Managing relationships (IE8) - Managing vision and purpose (IE9) - Motivating others (IE10) - Negotiating (IE11) - Personal learning and development (IE12) - Valuing diversity (IE13)	- Comfort around authority (OrS1) - Organizational agility (OrS2) - Presentation skills (OrS3) - Written communications (OrS4)	- Assessing talent (C1) - Conflict management (C2) - Managerial courage (C3)	- Action oriented (R1) - Drive for results (R2)	- Creativity (SS1) - Dealing with ambiguity (SS2) - Decision quality and problem solving (SS3) - Functional/technical skills (SS4) - Intellectual acumen (SS5) - Learning on the fly (SS6) - Strategic agility and innovation management (SS7) - Technical learning (SS8)	- Developing others (OpS1) - Directing others (OpS2) - Managing and measuring work (OpS3) - Managing through processes and systems (OpS4) - Organizing (OpS5) - Planning (OpS6) - Priority setting (OpS7) - Time management (OpS8) - Timely decision making (OpS9)

Table 1 presents the six qualities, or success factors, and its competencies. The factors can be divided into two categories: hard and soft skills. This categorization became usual as the hard skills are teachable abilities or skill sets that are easier to quantify, and the soft skills are subjective skills that are much harder to quantify.

For this categorization, we can consider as soft skills the core skill-sets: Individual Excellency, Courage, Results, Strategic Skills, and as hard skills the others: Operating Skills and Organizational Skills. This group of soft skills provides the ability to achieve results by working effectively with others in various circumstances; the ability to speak directly, honestly, and with respect in difficult situations; an emphasis on goal-oriented action; and an array of skills used to accomplish focused, long-term goals. As for the hard skills group, this provides an array of skills used for daily management of tasks and relationships; and the ability to communicate by various means within different organizational settings.

2.2 Game Genres

Games can be organized into categories (game genres) defined by the type of game play challenges (mechanics). Understanding games genres allows game designers to appropriately match new problems with a standard solution and to expand already established game mechanics [11]. The main factor that unifies a game genre is a similarity in the type of interaction that is supported between the player and the game [12]. So this interaction corresponds, to the game mechanics, as actions of game objects and players during the game play. These repeated actions or challenges are what defines the genre of a game.

Overall, this type of classification can be seen as a subjective practice, and the number of accepted game genres has evolved in recent years as games mechanics become more sophisticated and diverse [13]. Based on several available taxonomies of game genres [11, 14, 15], there isn't a standard, but rather a list which varies between 5 and 9 categories, which includes several sub-genres.

3 Relation Between Game Genres and Competences

In order to help the game designer to adapt the mechanics for a more effective training and certification through SG, the definition of game genre is one of the key points. For this reason, a study was developed to analyse the most common choices on the specific challenges used according to the competency sets [19]. For that an extended game genre taxonomy was used. This taxonomy is composed of eight sets: Action, Strategy, Playing, Sports, Management Simulation, Adventure, Puzzle and Quiz [16–18].

This game survey of 116 SG crossed the game genre categories with the previous sets of competences and as the results of this sampling we can identify some areas with significant identified intersections [19] in order to achieve the learning outcomes. This analysis is intended to identify the set of genres, from which the mechanics and challenges are more appropriate according to the core skills-set. The quantitative results obtained were based on a two-step approach. Firstly, we choosed the most relevant sub-genre of each game genre and compared them with each other, producing the results that allow the understanding on the distance between them. Secondly, the analysis falls on each chosen genre in comparison with all skills of Educational Competency Wheel. The results show how distinct impacts each game genre has in each skills training and can be used as knowledge to improve serious games design.

The potential of several game genres to support skill learning is extremely important and contributes to the development of a wide variety of strategies to the game design. This contribution can result in a mix of game genres or reinforcement of challenges to achieve skills such as: Decision Quality and Problem Solving and Technical Learning (SS); Organizing and Timely Decision Making (OpS); as well both skills results (Action Oriented and Drive for Results) can be synchronized with different strategies to get better learner performances.

Unfortunately, others skill sets haven't shown to be relevant, such as Individual Excellency, which shoes that the soft skills or personal development issues are more difficult either to train or to measure, in order to improve new skills. Exceptionally, the

Role. Playing Game genre presents several contributions in cooperative work (Building Effective Teams (IE), Motivating Others (IE) or Conflict Management (C)).

Table 2 presents which skill sets (hard and soft) are more appropriate for each game genre. Each column of skill type presents the most relevant skills-sets identified, and in some cases, one or more specific skills that distinguishes themselves.

Table 2. Summary of Games genre and Skills by genre and sub-genre

Genres	Sub-Genre	Hard skills	Soft skills
Action	Platform games		(R1) (SS3; SS7)
Strategy	Turn – based strategy	(OrS2) (OpS)	(SS) (R)
Role Playing	MMORPGs		(R) (C) (IE10; E11) (SS2; SS3; SS4)
Sports	Sport/Management games	(OpS5; OpS6; OpS3) (Or2)	(C3) (SS3) (R)
Management Simulation	Virtual worlds/Pets	(OrS2) (OpS)	(SS) (R)
Adventure	Graphics adventure	(OpS5)	(SS3; SS5; SS9) (R)
Puzzle	Action/Arcade puzzle (timed)	(OpS9)	(SS3; SS5; SS9)
Quizzes			(SS9)

The set of graphical analysis presented in [19] demonstrate the stronger correlation and impact between some game genres, such as adventure, sport, strategy and management simulation, and some of the hard skills (organizational and operating) and soft skills (strategic and results). An expected result is the low impact of most game genres with the core skills-set of Intellectual Excellency, with the exception of RPG.

4 Methodology for In-Game Certification

Rather than evaluating the players' performance at the end of the game using traditional questionnaire forms, we propose a four steps design methodology for in-game certification [20]. We provide a set of guidelines for game designers to build games for the competence certification, and an in-game assessment framework. This is needed to balance the relationship between the game mechanics for serious game genres, the array of competences to certify, and the game elements.

Following this methodology, we'll first get the diagnosis of training context through to identify the situations, applied scenarios as well as its objectives. Secondly, the competency profiles of the training target groups must be defined. In this step, the Education Competences, as seen in Table 1, serves as a reference to identify which (or the combination of) competencies should be used to obtain the correct outcomes for each scenario. This tool helps building the mapping of a restricted and adequate number of competencies (core competencies), based on expected results.

Thirdly, the game designer selects the basic mechanics by matching the list of competencies identified on the previous step to the correlation matrix (available at https://db.tt/Sl9JBACM) and summarized in Table 2 [19]. Lastly, the forth step is to obtain the triadic certification model (Fig. 1) with the following axes: the identified skills (competences), mechanics based on game genres (mechanics) and training levels (play). Similarly with the Triadic Game Design [21], the balancing between the three components is the success of the certification process, which is supported through the Analytics.

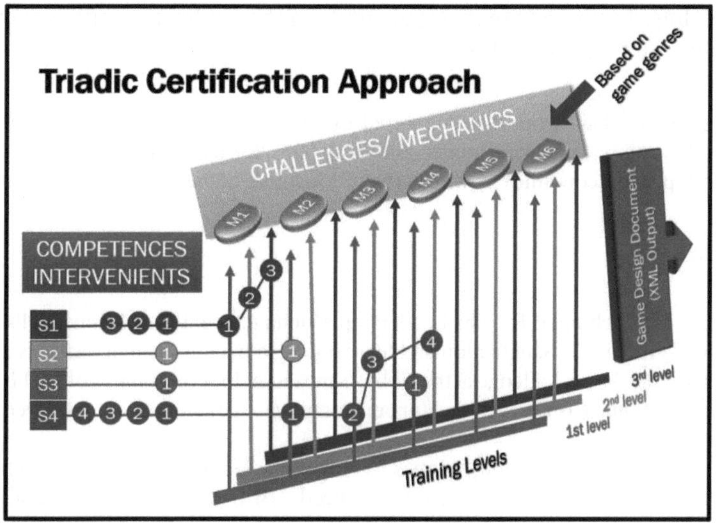

Fig. 1. The triadic certification model

This approach keeps each process independent to each intervenient: trainer(s) (who define the training competences), game designer(s) (who define game elements of serious game) and certification (how to analyse the training data). This is a starting point and the suggested mechanics are the directions and procedures that professionals will further develop to enliven the user experience.

5 Conclusions and Future Work

In the future, the game genres survey will be continuously updated with the analysis of new releases of SG, in order to improve the best game genre identification to achieve the desired learning outcomes. This contribution may eventually be developed as game genres vs competence and skill matrix.

The Serious Games emerge as an interesting alternative for training and certification of competences because they can offer a more meaningful and engaging learning experience. While desirable to measure the performance as a whole and through the game, by applying the in-game certification methodology, the results allow, both individually and combined, the quantification of player performance based on the competence matrix.

With this methodology approach in generic game we intend to define, verify and validate the game design contributions and how systems are capable to provide effective learning experiences. The success of this proof of concept is defined by the player performance results into different training itineraries.

The results of the analysis of the relation between game genres and competences show that can be applied as reference to different training contexts or domain areas, as well as how it can be useful to understand previous experiences and can provide hints for the game designers to develop new SG. Future work will also focus on integrating this methodology in several areas. An example of the application of this methodology to the tourism can be seen in [20].

Acknowledgments. This work was supported by the project "New Tools for Certification in Game-based Learning" financed under the Call for Research Proposals on Innovation, Entrepreneurship, and Economic Growth by the IC2 Institute of the University of Texas at Austin.

References

1. Lombardo, M., Eichinger, R.: The Leadership Machine. Lominger, Minneapolis (2005)
2. Jegers, K., Wiberg, C.: Satisfaction and learnability in edutainment: a usability study of the knowledge game laser challenge at the Noble e-museum. In: Proceedings of HCI International – 10th International Conference on Human Computer Interaction, Crete, Greece, pp. 1096–1102, June 2003
3. Freitas, S., Jarvis, S.: Serious games – engaging training solutions: a research and development project for supporting training needs. Brit. J. Educ. Technol. **38**(3), 523–525 (2007)
4. Yang, Y.: Building virtual cities, inspiring intelligent citizens: digital games for developing students' problem solving and learning motivation. Comput. Educ. **59**, 365–377 (2012)
5. Michael, D., Chen, S.: Serious Games: Games That Educate, Train and Inform. Thomson, Boston (2006)
6. Bergeron, B.: Developing Serious Games. Thomson Delmar Learning, Boston (2006)
7. Baptista, R, Coelho, A, and Vaz de Carvalho, C.: Location-based tourism in-game certification. In: Proceedings of 9th International Technology, Education and Development Conference (INTED 2015), Madrid, Spain, pp. 3602–3610 (2015)
8. Constant Contact: Lominger Standard 67 Competencies and Related Descriptions (2014). http://library.constantcontact.com/download/get/file/1107007864445-56/Lominger +Competencies.pdf
9. Garman, A., Johnson, M.: Leadership competences: an introduction. J. Healthcare Manag. **51**(1), 13–17 (2006)
10. Microsoft. Education Competencies Information from Microsoft for Teachers and School Leaders (2006). http://www.microsoft.com/en-us/education/training-and-events/education-competencies/default.aspx#fbid=mwuu8jS9xBZ?Competencies
11. Adams, E., Rollings, A.: Fundamentals of Game Design. Prentice Hall, Upper Saddle River (2006)
12. Pinelle, D., Wong, N., Stach, T.: Using genres to customize usability evaluations of video games. In: Proceedings of the 2008 Conference on Future Play: Research, Play, Share (Future Play 2008), pp. 129–136. ACM, New York (2008)
13. Sellers, M.: Designing the experience of interactive play. In: Vorderer, P., Bryant, J. (eds.) Playing Video Games: Motives, Responses, Consequences. Lawrence Erlbaum Associates, Mahwah (2006)

14. Bateman, C., Boon, R.: 21st Century Game Design. Charles River Media, Inc., Hingham (2006)
15. Stahl, T.: Video Games Genres. http://www.thocp.net/software/games/reference/genres.htm
16. Adams, E., Dormans, J.: Game Mechanics: Advanced Game Design. New Riders, Berkeley (2012)
17. Entertainment Software Association: Essential Facts about the Computer and Video Game Industry 2011. http://www.theesa.com/facts/pdfs/ESA_EF_2011.pdf
18. Wolf, M.: Genre and the video game. In: The Medium of the Video Game. University of Texas Press (2001). http://www.robinlionheart.com/gamedev/genres.xhtml
19. Baptista, R., Coelho, A., Vaz de Carvalho, C.: Relation between game genres and competence development – contributions to serious game design. In: Proceedings of 9th European Conference on Games Based Learning ECGBL 2015, Steinkjer, Norway (2015)
20. Baptista, R., Gonçalves, R., Coelho, A., Vaz de Carvalho, C.: Methodology for creating a competences certification correlation matrix. In: Proceedings of ICERI 2013 Conference, 18th–20th November 2013, Seville, Spain, pp. 2522–2535 (2014)
21. Harteveld, C.: Triadic Game Design: Balancing Reality, Meaning, and Play. Springer, London, p. 316 (2011)

Serious Games for the Cognitive Stimulation of Adults: A Proposal of a Pilot Project

Ricardo Alves[1(✉)], Teresa Souto[2], Paula Escudeiro[1,3], and Nuno Escudeiro[3,4]

[1] Games Interaction and Learning Technoogies - GILT, Porto, Portugal
ricalves03@gmail.com, pmo@isep.ipp.pt
[2] Faculty of Psychology, Education and Sports, Lusófona University of Porto, Porto, Portugal
p2683@ulp.pt
[3] Instituto Superior de Engenharia do Porto, Porto, Portugal
nfe@isep.ipp.pt
[4] Laboratory of Artificial Intelligence and Decision Support, INESC TEC, Porto, Portugal

Abstract. One of the major challenges for healthcare professionals in the XXI century is the increasing number of elderly in the world population. It is clearly important to find ways to stimulate cognitively this population, helping them to develop strategies and maintaining independency in their daily life activities. Conventional cognitive stimulation is time consuming task often causing discomfort in patients. Computer based tools may be used to perform cognitive stimulation and improve transferability in a setting that does not increase anxiety in individuals. This paper aims to present a pilot study of automatic platforms to enhance the cognitive process for older adults in order to promote an active aging.

Keywords: Pilot project · Virtual reality · Serious games · Active ageing · Cognitive processes

1 Introduction

It is anticipated that the number of individuals among the worldwide population, over the age of 60 "is expected to more than double, from 841 million people in 2013 to more than 2 billion in 2050" [1]. The increasing number of the elderly population is one of main challenges of the XXI century, being of utmost importance to invest in the field of aging, understanding how healthcare professionals can intervene, promoting an active ageing as an indispensable component to minimize the social and economic impact of this phenomenon. Active ageing is "the process of optimizing opportunities for health, participation and security in order to enhance quality of life as people age" [2]. Since aging is accompanied by changes in cognitive functioning in several areas [3], it is clearly important to find ways to stimulate cognitively this population, helping them to develop compensation strategies and maintaining independency in their daily life activities [4].

Automatic tools, based on computer technology, notably serious games, are becoming more common to support the assessment and intervention in cognitive

C. Vaz de Carvalho et al. (Eds.): SGAMES 2015, LNICST 161, pp. 36–41, 2016.
DOI: 10.1007/978-3-319-29060-7_7

processes. Serious games may simulate daily life scenarios where the user active role is designed to promote generalization and transferability thus, contributing to active aging.

In this paper we propose a serious game for dynamically monitoring the patient's cognitive abilities and adapting the game activities to the user specific needs.

In the remaining of this paper we review the state of the art in Sect. 2. In Sect. 3 we describe the proposed serious game and the evaluation methodology and in Sect. 4 we conclude.

2 Automatic Platforms

In recent years we have seen an increase attempt to identify ways to reduce and/or neutralize the progression of neurocognitive decline. This trend is largely based on the idea of cognitive plasticity [5]. Accordingly, cognitive stimulation, is being used to slow down cognitive decline, by reinforcing the functions relatively preserved [6, 7], using intervention programs [8], allowing the brain to change its structures and functions [9].

2.1 Applicability and Potential

The use of an automatic platform with guiding principles that supports both evaluative and psychoeducational approaches, as well as a programmed neurocognitive stimulation, based on an emerging methodology of stimuli presentation, the Serious Games (SG), is of utmost importance. SG are a generally accepted software interface created with the purpose of helping in the assessment and intervention, other than entertainment [10], that has been increasingly presented as an important resource for assessment and intervention in cognitive processes [10–13].

Conventional cognitive assessment is based on neuropsychological evaluation that is time consuming, expensive [14], and often causing embarrassment and discomfort in patients [15]. Being so, the use of new technologies as a procedure to assess cognitive function and functional deficits in this population [16] means developing tools aimed at reducing the cost and time associated with conventional methods [14] and also the introduction of a motivating element in interventions for this subjects [17].

The consolidation and expansion of this resource in multiple domains of human reality allowed important changes from education to intervention or training skills, as well as advances in new technologies targeted to improve life quality of individuals with special needs [12]. The resource to SG using Virtual Reality (VR) represents a scientific and technological development, and an important search for interactive interfaces that are closest to human senses. The VR ability to create dynamic and stimulating environments, aiming recovery of cognitive functions in which all behavioral responses can be registered, provides testing and training options otherwise impossible through traditional psychological methods [18].

2.2 Application in the Therapeutic Area

As a methodological resource, VR has a significant potential for cognitive evaluation and intervention in individuals with a diagnosis of incapacitating mental illness. VR facilitates access to stimulating exercises and tasks aimed at different skills (cognitive, motor) supported in virtual environments (VE) promoting significant association with individual's daily life tasks.

The potential of VE have been explored, highlighting the dynamic and motivational features that apply to recovery of cognitive functions, enables a methodical and exhaustive behavioral recording that represents a qualitatively improved alternative compared to traditional methodologies. Providing a flexible and controlled environment, VE are suitable to the use of multi-sensory channels, to be applied in experimental and therapeutic contexts [18].

The potential of this technology comes from its main features, including the possibility of user immersion in a perceptual world computer generated, i.e. the feeling of the subject that there is really (presence), the possibility of interaction with the environment in real time, giving the subject an active role and greater involvement by ensuring the ecological validity [19, 20]. VE enable a specialized support in recovery process, as it promotes generalization of activities/tasks trained [21, 22] and possibly catalysis the transference procedure [21–23].

2.3 The Use of Serious Games with Older Adults

The use of SG with older people is still in a premature phase [24]. However, previous studies show that SG will have an important impact in the prevention and rehabilitation of older people [25]. Multiple positive uses for VR previously described, and the empiric evidence that SG can be used with promising results in this population provides an incentive to pursue scientific research in this domain. SG can enhance through solving attractive tasks, the contexts needed for repeating tasks, feedback and background processing [25]. Despite a number of studies that point to difficulties regarding subjects getting familiar with the game technology [19], and problems interacting with SG [26], those difficulties derive from the fact that a majority of these SG were not created for this specific population. To overcome this problem, specific SG are emerging that follow specific guidelines especially suitable for older adults [10].

3 Serious Games: A Pilot Project

The pilot project is currently being developed at GILT *(*Games, Interaction and Learning Technologies*)* by a multidisciplinary team aiming the creation of an automatic platform for cognitive assessment and training that can be used to implement individualized interventions and respective assessment (taking into count the limitations of the subject and symptoms).

The platform methodological construction options consider, in the program, a complete evaluation procedure. To build the evaluation module, it is important to appeal for planned use of tools and methods, using the amendments that enable the project presentation on time and the evaluation module must also allow running a study on the relevance and effectiveness of the stimuli that will be carried out.

The program intervention must have a modular structure so it can promote generalization and transference to the individual's real life context, respecting one's rhythm and also creating interactions in a secure environment, where the user's anxiety levels will be minimized. Being so, it increases user's motivation and, at the same time, encourages task practice. The use of these interactive components enables the management and manipulation of different elements - stimuli setting, congruence among others. The user-specialist can structure and set modules to specific interventions. The program should also be able to keep track of the patient's cognitive abilities, to monitored goals/ purposes and to adapt the difficulty level of game to the user. Finally, be able to promote ecological interactions [26, 27] and facilitate the generalization and transference processes.

In this application, it will be required that no latencies or graphic inconsistencies occur and, simultaneously, that the three-dimensionality is congruently assured.

Several usability tests will be conducted, using multiple users. Their comments and remarks will be carefully registered. Experimental tests will be held to ensure the back office and application effectiveness.

Adjustments will be made during the test phase of the trial version of the application in order to blur the possible resistance in the use of the equipment and application. The devices will be chosen considering effectiveness, but also the perception of user's comfort.

In the final evaluation stage we will support the assessment of the cognitive function on several common scientific tests. We will use reference tests [28] such as WAIS-III, MoCA - Montreal Cognitive Assessment, STROOP, TMT - Trail Making Test, REY 15 Item Memory Test, California Verbal Learning Test.

4 Conclusion

If the beneficial effects of SG are demonstrated by robust studies, the potential social impact is huge considering: high prevalence of cognitive impairment and popularity of video games among future subjects in risk of cognitive decline. SG can be an attractive way and a sustainable method for improving or at least delay the neurocognitive decline, sensory-motor, psychosocial and emotional of the elderly [26]. After validated, platform for cognitive assessment and training can constitute a powerful screening tool for the early detection of cognitive impairment and the stored data can be collected, not only to estimate parameters that reflect cognitive processes, but also to monitor neuropsychological profiles and improve the intervention.

References

1. United Nations. World Population Ageing 2013 [Internet]. Department of Economic and Social Affairs, Population Division, New York, USA. Report No.: ST/ESA/SER.A/348 (2013). http://www.un.org/en/development/desa/population/publications/pdf/ageing/WorldPopulationAgeing2013.pdf
2. World Health Organization. Active Ageing: a Policy Framework. A Contribution of the World Health Organization to the Second United Nations World Assembly on Ageing, Madrid, Spain, April 2002. http://whqlibdoc.who.int/hq/2002/WHO_NMH_NPH_02.8.pdf
3. Glisky, E.: Changes in cognitive function in human aging. In: Riddle, D.R. (ed.) Brain Aging: Models, Methods, and Mechanisms. CRC Press, Boca Raton (2007)
4. American Psychiatric Association: Diagnostic and Statistical Manual of Mental Disorders, 5th edn. American Psychiatric Publishing, Arlington (2013)
5. Mayas, J., Parmentier, F., Andrés, P., Ballesteros, S.: Plasticity of attentional functions in older adults after non-action video game training: a randomized controlled trial. PLoS ONE **9**(3), 1–11 (2014)
6. La Rue, A.: Healthy brain aging: role of cognitive reserve, cognitive stimulation and cognitive. Clin. Geriatr. Med. **26**, 99–111 (2010). (A. K. Desai, Ed.)
7. Spector, A., Orrell, M., Woods, B.: Cognitive stimulation to improve cognitive functioning in people with dementia. Int. J. Geriatr. Psychiatry **25**(12), 1253–1258 (2010)
8. Coltheart, M.: Assumptions and methods in cognitive neuropsychology. In: Rapp, B. (ed.) Handbook of Cognitive Neuropsychology: What Deficits Reveal About the Human Mind, pp. 3–21. Psychology Press, Philadelphia (2000)
9. Duffau, H.: Brain plasticity: from pathophysiological mechanisms to therapeutic applications. J. Clin. Neurosci. **13**(9), 885–897 (2006)
10. Robert, P.H., König, A., Amieva, H., et al.: Recommendations for the use of serious games in people with Alzheimer's disease, related disorders and frailty. Front. Aging Neurosci. **6**(54), 1–13 (2014). doi:10.3389/fnagi.2014.00054
11. Riva, G., Rizzo, A., Alpini, D., et al.: Virtual environments in the diagnosis, prevention and intervention of age-related diseases: a review of VR scenarios proposed in the EC VETERAN Project. Cyberpsychol Behav. **2**, 577–591 (1999)
12. Rizzo, A., Wiederhold, M., Buckwalter, J.: Basic issues in the use of virtual environments for mental health application. In: Riva, G., Wiederhold, B.K., Molinari, E. (eds.) Virtual Environments in Clinical Psychology and Neuroscience, pp. 21–42. Ios Press, Amsterdam (1998)
13. Cherniack, E.P.: Not just fun and games: applications of virtual reality in the identification and rehabilitation of cognitive disorders of the elderly. Disabil. Rehabil. Assist. Technol. **6**, 283–289 (2011). doi:10.3109/17483107.2010.542570
14. Zucchella, C., Sinforiani, E., Tassorelli, C., et al.: Serious games for screening pre-dementia conditions: from virtuality to reality? A pilot project. Funct. Neurol. **29**(3), 153–158 (2014)
15. Segal, R., Bhatia, M., Drapeau, M.: Therapist's perception of benefits and costs of using virtual reality treatments. Cyberpsychology, Behav. Soc. Networking **14**(1–2), 29–34 (2011)
16. Tarnanas, I., Tsolaki, M., Nef, T., et al.: Can a novel computerized cognitive screening test provide additional information for early detection of Alzheimer's disease? Alzheimers Dement. **10**, 790–798 (2014). doi:10.1016/j.jalz.2014.01.002
17. Anguera, J.A., Boccanfuso, J., Rintoul, J.L., Al-Hashimi, et al.: Video game training enhances cognitive control in older adults. Nature **501**, 97–102 (2013). doi:10.1038/nature12486

18. Costa, R., Carvalho, L.: Experimentando um Ambiente Virtual com Pacientes Neuropsiquiátricos. II Conferência Internacional de Tecnologias de Informação e Comunicação na Educação - Challenges 2001, pp. 529–546, Braga (2001)
19. Rizzo, A.A., Kim, G.J.: A SWOT analysis of the field of VR rehabilitation and therapy. Presence Teleoper. Virtual Environ. **14**, 119–146 (2005). doi:10.1162/1054746053967094
20. Dyck, M., Winbeck, M., Leiberg, S., et al.: Recognition profile of emotions in natural and virtual faces. PLoS ONE **3**(11), e3268, 1–8 (2008)
21. Wendt, G.W.: Tecnologias de interface humano-computacional: realidade virtual e novos caminhos para pesquisa. Revista de Psiquiatria Clinica **38**(5), 211–212 (2011)
22. Costa, R.: Ambientes Virtuais na Reabilitação Cognitiva de Pacientes Neurológicos e Psiquiátricos. UFRJ, Rio de Janeiro (2000)
23. Jerônimo, R.A., Lima, S.: Tecnologias Computacionais e ambientes virtuais no processo terapêutico de reabilitação. O mundo da Saúde **30**(1), 96–106 (2006)
24. Alzheimer's Disease International: World Alzheimer Report 2014: Dementia and Risk Reduction: An Analysis of Protective and Modifiable Factors. Alzheimer's Disease International, London (2014)
25. Muscio, C., Tiraboschi, P., Guerra, U.P., et al.: Clinical trial design of serious gaming in mild cognitive impairment. Front. Aging Neurosci. **7**(26), 1–6 (2015). doi:10.3389/fnagi.2015.00026
26. Wiemeyer, J., Kliem, A.: Serious games in prevention and rehabilitation – a new panacea for elderly people? Eur. Rev. Aging Phys. Act. **9**, 41–50 (2012). doi:10.1007/s11556-011-0093-x
27. Souto, T., Baptista, A., Tavares, D., et al.: Facial emotional recognition in schizophrenia: preliminary results of the virtual reality program for facial emotional recognition. Rev. Psiq. Clín. **40**(4), 129–134 (2013)
28. Simões, M.R.: Instrumentos de avaliação psicológica de pessoas idosas: investigação e estudos de validação em Portugal. RIDEP **34**(1), 9–33 (2012)

VirtualSign in Serious Games

Paula Escudeiro(✉), Nuno Escudeiro, Marcelo Norberto, and Jorge Lopes

Departamento de Engenharia Informática, Instituto Superior de Engenharia do Porto, Porto, Portugal
{pmo,nfe,matno,jolbl}@isep.ipp.pt

Abstract. This paper presents the game developed within the VirtualSign project. This game aims to make the process of learning sign language easier and enjoyable. In the game the player can control an avatar and interact with several objects and Non-player characters in order to obtain signs. To obtain those signs the player will have to overcome challenges and use the VirtualSign Translator. The player then has to perform the gesture himself and information is sent from the translator to the game. This improves the interactivity and makes the game more interesting and motivating. The game has as an inventory system where the signs are kept and can be checked. This lets the user visualize and learn or train the various existing configurations of gestures. There are also various checkpoints to check the player acquired knowledge, a highscore list and a continuous storyline.

Keywords: VirtualSign · Serious games · Portuguese Sign Language · Kinect

1 Introduction

Games have become a recognized way of providing rich content to its players, especially digital games. Digital games provide a remarkable opportunity to overcome the lack of educational digital content available for the hearing impaired community. Playing a game as the name suggest has a great leisure aspect that can't be found in conventional educational means. Educational game researcher Gee [1] shows how good game designers manage to get new players to learn their long, complex, and difficult games. A well-designed game entices players into the "reality" of the game world and keeps them there until the goals of the game have been met [2]. Making these opportunities available to those who endure handicap and disabilities is a core concern in today's society and a must to promote equity and inclusion. In this work we propose a new approach by using a game to make the process of learning sign language enjoyable and interactive. In this game the player controls a character that interacts with various objects and non-player characters with the aim of collecting several gestures from the Portuguese Sign Language. The game is played in first person view in which the player controls a character on the map. Each map represents a level and each level has several objects that represent signs scattered through the map for the player to interact with. All objects obtained by the player will be stored in his inventory and can be accessed at any point during the game. With these objects the player can then perform the gesture at the

C. Vaz de Carvalho et al. (Eds.): SGAMES 2015, LNICST 161, pp. 42–49, 2016.
DOI: 10.1007/978-3-319-29060-7_8

checkpoint using the VirtualSign Translator or they can chose to play without the translator in which case the avatar will be the one performing the gestures.

2 State of the Art

There are some projects related to this theme/area but none of them implies an automatic bidirectional translation process in a game as this does, therefor, making this project very innovative. There is a rising number of serious games projects. Some of the most relevant related works within the sign language scope are described below.

The game *CopyCat* [3] is the most similar project in comparison to ours. It consists of a game where sign language gestures need to be executed properly in order to proceed. The movement analysis is done through gloves with sensors. However, the researchers from the *CopyCat* project have published a video where they show their intention to use Kinect for movement detection. Their current research platform is a custom system that uses computer vision, colored gloves and wrist-mounted 3-axis accelerometers. These are used to collect data as users sign and machine learning to recognize the signs for game play. The system was built on top of Ubuntu Linux and uses the Kinect system as input for the computer vision, which replaces the gloves and sensors.

ProDeaf is an application that does the translation of Portuguese text or voice to Brazilian gesture language. This project is not a serious game but it is very similar to one of the main components used on the VirtualSign game, which is the text to gesture translation. The objective of the ProDeaf is to make the communication between mute and deaf people easier by making digital content accessible in Brazilian gesture language. The translation is done using a 3D avatar that performs the gestures. This software is already used by over 130 000 users.

Kinect Sign Language Translator is another project that is similar to the VirtualSign Translator. The project was a result of collaboration, facilitated by Microsoft Research, between the Chinese Academy of Sciences, Beijing Union University, and Microsoft Research Asia, each of which made crucial contributions. Dedicated researchers in China have created the Kinect Sign Language Translator, a prototype system that understands the gestures of sign language and converts them to spoken and written language—and vice versa. The system captures a conversation from both sides: it displays the signer and renders a written and spoken translation of the sign language in real-time, and it also takes the non-signer's spoken words and turns them into accurate, understandable sign language. An avatar on the screen represents the non-signer and makes the appropriate sign languages gestures.

3 The Game

The VirtualSign game aims to teach Portuguese Sign Language (PSL) in the most enjoyable and motivational way. Therefore, the creation of the game had a series of factors to consider, how the gameplay should be to reach this goal and which structure the game should have. Below are the most important aspects of the game.

3.1 Gameplay

The gameplay is the most important part of the game. This aspect can increase or decrease how much the user will to play the game, as the game designer David Perry said: *Keep the gameplay challenging, but don't let players get lost or blame the game for their problems. A good game designer always knows what the player is thinking and looking over their shoulder every step of the way.* [4]

In order to keep the game challenging there is a score system as well as a storyline so that the player feels motivated when performing a task. The score is based on the time the user spends to achieve a goal, which may be clearing a checkpoint or finding a sign. The signs are spread out around the scenes and the player will need to find them with the help from the Non-Player Characters (NPC) and a map with hints. There is also always a minimap in the corner of the screen to help the player stay oriented. There are two types of checkpoints, the first type is the one required to gain access to the next area of the scene and usually requires a set of signs. The other type only requires a single sign and is used to gain another different sign. The second type of checkpoint is required to finish a level but the user can choose the order in which to clear it. Some of the gestures will also trigger minigames with score systems as well where the user will acquire a gesture depending on his score [5].

The game starts by showing the user an interface explaining the basics of the game and introduces the story. The character is told by a friendly NPC that he must find someone and in order to do so he will need to collect all the gestures. Then after introducing his name the player can start his adventure in an open world scene. All the interactive items always give feedback and this feedback is always either hints for the player or a part of the story. The story has a relevant mysterious aspect to it. We tried to make sure that the story gives hints so that the player starts to realize what is happening in the virtual word but never being clear enough so that he loses interest in the story [6]. When the player acquires a sign that sign is added to his inventory, this inventory is where the user can access and see all his gestures at any time. The avatar is capable of

Fig. 1. Avatar in the first level, the score can be seen on the top, and on the corners there is the timer *(top)* and the minimap *(bottom)*. The image also shows the inventory containing three gestures *(three square images with hand configurations)* and the avatar is performing the C sign.

representing all the hand configurations of Portuguese Sign Language, meaning all the letters and numbers as well as a selected set of words and sentences. To see the avatar performing the gesture the player simply needs to click the desired gesture. After each level there is an evaluation scenario where the player's knowledge will be evaluated to check if the information is being retained by the player. In those scenes there is a NPC that will ask the player to perform certain signs, however, contrary to the checkpoints in the level, the user will not be able to access his inventory and check which gesture represents what (Fig. 1).

3.2 Scenarios

The game has three main scenarios as well as three evaluation ones. The scenarios were built in accordance to the game plot [7]. The first one is the one where the player can obtain letters and numbers and it takes place in a desert. There are three main checkpoints where the player must perform the gestures and only after passing those checkpoints the player can access the next area of the scenario.

The second scenario is where the player starts to learn words and has to use them to acquire new gestures. It also has checkpoints, however, unlike the first where there were three checkpoints where the player had to perform six gestures in each, on this second level the player only has to perform one word per checkpoint.

As for the third and last scenario, we used the scenario provided by one of Unity assets and added the NPCs and objects needed, the logic of this scene is just as the second level except that instead using words we are now using full sentences.

Other than these three main scenes there is the starting menu, the evaluation levels and mini-games (Fig. 2).

Fig. 2. Three main scenarios of the game. The alphabet *(left)*, word *(middle)* and sentences *(right)* scenarios generic view.

4 Technical Aspects

Several technical aspects had to be taken into consideration to successfully develop this game, as it involves a number of different technologies and a connection to the Virtual-Sign Translator application. The game was developed in Unity 3D which is a game development software and some of the models as well as the main avatar were created and animated on Blender. Below there is a more deeply insight on those aspects.

4.1 Requirements

The functional requirements identified early in the project were:

- Start Menu where the player can choose the type of game he wants (with or without Kinect), consult the options or exit;
- Menu options where you can change the graphics quality, volume, save or load the game and see the table of high scores;

The game requirements within the levels are:

- Handling and control of the character;
- Interact with NPCs (Non-Player Characters);
- Consult the inventory and use the items in it;
- Interaction with map objects;
- Access to the above options menu;
- Access the mini-games;

As for the Non-Functional requirements the usability [8], adaptability and performance were the main focus. This project aims to be fairly intuitive, allowing easy adaptation and learning. The interfaces were developed with the care to enable a pleasant interaction. The character controls were also structured to present a simple usage. Along the game there are several short explanations of how the player should act to fulfil the objectives and surpass the levels. Every interactive object or NPC gives the player some kind of feedback. The gaming performance is a factor of the utmost importance, any perceptive delay can affect the gameplay making the game annoying rather than fun. To maintain the performance this game was tested to never run less than 60 frames per second on an optimal computer. The ideal frame rate for a game must be around 40 frames per second [9]. The essential functions are constantly executed and the code are optimized to avoid the waste of resources.

Besides the code all the factors that constrain the performance of the game are taken into account, such as textures, bumps, number of vertices of the 3D models among others. As for the gesture recognition the VirtualSign Translator works in real time with no delay nor is there any delay in the connection between the translator and the game so the input from the player performing the gestures is instantaneous and can be seen on the interface at the checkpoints. In terms of adaptability the scripting was thought and created as templates so that they can be changed in case there's the need to increase the sign count or even adding a new language. The only issue with the adaptability is the animations for the new words and new language that must be created and imported. However, this was also thought so the avatar animations are separate from the avatar itself and the animation created with a similar skeleton can be played by it.

4.2 Game Layers

Given its high degree of complexity the game was divided into layers. At the top level there is the interface. All the functionalities of the project can be accessed through this layer by the user. This layer is responsible for the transmission of the actions of the user for the following layers. On the lower level there are three layers. The sockets layer which is responsible for linking Unity to the VirtualSign Translator application. The game engine layer that represents Unity [10] and the business layer (Fig. 3).

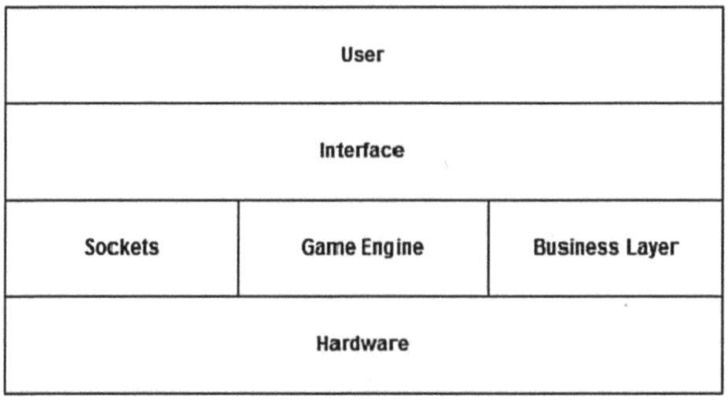

Fig. 3. Application architecture layers.

4.3 Scripting

All the scripts were developed considering the performance and adaptability [11] of the game. Below there are descriptions of some of the main functionalities. One of the most important scripts is the inventory one, the inventory contains a list of signs, each sign contains an id and string of the sign meaning. The inventory icons on the interface are obtained based on the id of each item, therefor, making the inventory adjustable. Example of the method used to add items to the inventory:

```
public void addItem(int ID, string gesture){
Item item_ = new Item(ID,textures[ID],gesture);
GameObject item = (GameObject)Instantiate(inventoryItem);
Button b = item.GetComponent<Button>();
b.onClick.AddListener(() => ItemClicked(ID));
RawImage raw = item.GetComponent<RawImage> ();
raw.texture = textures[ID];
itens_gui.Add (item);
itens.Add (item_);
inv.score.setScore(inv.CheckTimer,timer.getTimer());
inv.CheckTimer.setTimeC(timer.getTimer());}
```

The score is incremented when the user finds a gesture as it can be seen on the code above. The information containing the current time (timer) and the time where the last gesture was found (CheckTimer) are sent to a setScore method that will calculate the score based on the difference of times. After the score is set the CheckTimer is updated to the current time.

Another crucial part of the scripting is the connection to the VirtualSign Translator.

Since the gesture to text translator is a separate and complex application developed in C it was easier to connect to it than to integrate it in the game as the game is being developed in Unity 3D using C#. Therefor a socket based connection was created between the game and the translator. The connection is only created at checkpoints where the player will be asked to perform the gesture. The translator sends the translated information to the game in real time, there was never any noticeable delay. On the game side, as soon as the string containing the detected translation arrives it is shown in the checkpoint interface.

The other main component is the translation from text, which in the game corresponds to the items the player acquires, into gestures. To assure the adaptability of the game, the avatar has a list of animations and those animations are sorted by the id of the corresponding sign. The animations are separate from the avatar and they can be simply dragged into the list of animation of the avatar and he will have access to them. The only restriction on this matter is that the animation must be created with a similar skeleton structure to the one from the avatar. As for the interaction within the game with the virtual world, all the interactive items and NPCs have colliders and when the player enters them it will show an option to interact by pressing the E key. If the player presses the key there will always be some kind of feedback. This happens because we developed template scripts that can be adjusted so new information can be added easily.

5 Conclusion

The implications for understanding the relationship between games and learning are that games need not be defined as an essential instrument or a type of content but as contemporary human creations whose forms and meanings are strategic for education, more specifically concerning the hearing impaired community. The selection of this target population is due to the growing number of students with special needs who complete both elementary and high school and come to higher education. This situation demands for new means that allow these individuals to have easy access to educational digital content. In order to motivate them towards the learning process we have created a game that combines the sign language learning process with the pleasant feeling of playing a digital game. We believe this is a great time to take on the challenge of adopting new digital media, serious games and interactive simulations. However, the development of a game is always a complex task and many adversities were faced along the way. A lot of effort and time was needed to face challenges and solve problems, but a fair amount of knowledge was acquired during this process. As for future work the game can be adapted for mobile platforms [12]. Also as the game is on its final stage of development a quantitative evaluation framework has been created and the next step will be to fill it based on tests from users.

References

1. Gee, J.P.: What Video Games Have to Teach Us About Learning and Literacy. Palgrave Macmillan, New York (2003)
2. Salen, K., Zimmerman, E.: Rules of Play: Game Design Fundamentals. MIT Press, Cambridge, MA (2004)
3. Perry, D.: Saltzman, p. 24 (1999)
4. Georgia Institute of Technology. http://cats.gatech.edu/content/copycat
5. Creighton, R.H.: Unity 3D Game Development by Example: A Seat-of-Your-Pants Manual for Building Fun, Groovy Little Games Quickly. Packt Publishing Ltd, Birmingham (2010)
6. Schell, J.: Understanding entertainment: story and gameplay are one. Comput. Entertainment (CIE) **3**(1), 6 (2005)
7. Mariais, C., Michau, F., Pernin, J.P.: The use of game principles in the design of learning role-playing game scenarios. In: Proceedings of the ECGBL 2010, pp. 462–469 (2010)
8. Holm, I.: Ideas and Beliefs in Architecture and Industrial Design: How Attitudes, Orientations, and Underlying Assumptions Shape the Built Environment. Oslo School of Architecture and Design, Oslo (2006)
9. Claypool, K.T., Claypool, M.: On frame rate and player performance in first person shooter games. Multimedia Syst. **13**(1), 3–17 (2007)
10. Goldstone, W.: Unity Game Development Essentials. Packt Publishing Ltd., Birmingham (2009)
11. Ketfi, A., Belkhatir, N.: Dynamic interface adaptability in service oriented software. In: 8th International Workshop on Component-Oriented Programming (WCOP 2003), Darmstadt, Germany, July 2003
12. Jie, J., Yang, K., Haihui, S.: Research on the 3D game scene optimization of mobile phone based on the unity 3D engine. In: 2011 International Conference on Computational and Information Sciences (ICCIS), pp. 875–877. IEEE, October 2011

The Design and Study of a Serious Game for Attention Training of the Older Adults

Chun-Hsiang Ku, Shwu-Lih Huang, and Tsai-Yen Li(✉)

National Chengchi University, 64, Sec. 2, Zhi-Nan Rd, Taipei, Taiwan
{99753012,slh,li}@nccu.edu.tw

Abstract. In this research, we have designed a parameterizable serious game on tablet computer to study how such a system can improve the attention of the older adults. In the experiments, we have adopted two types of tests: Visual Search (VS) and Attention Network Test (ANT) as the pretests and posttests. In the game sessions, we have incorporated visual search exercises in the game to provide attention trainings for the older adults. The experimental results show that some cognitive abilities of the participants can be significantly improved, and most of the subjects are willing to continue to play the game after the experiments. The design of our serious game succeeded in achieving the goal of attention training for the older adults.

Keywords: Game-based learning · Cognitive abilities · Parameterization · Older adults · Attention

1 Introduction

Many countries are facing the problem of becoming an aging society. The percentage of older adults with declined cognitive abilities is increasing. The goal of our system is to design a serious game to improve the attention of the older adults. Due to the declined cognitive abilities of the older adults, it is crucial to design a game that can not only increase their motivation but also serve the purpose of attention training. As revealed in the study of Slegers [7], compared to the younger generations, the older adults have a stronger preference of games over other computer application software (such as word processing, email, and web browsers). Therefore, in this work, we aim to design a game-based learning system for the older adults to perform attention training. In order to lower the barrier of playing a game for the older adults, we have taken advantage of the intuitive user interface provided by a tablet computer to design our serious game. We conduct experiments to study how this kind of serious game can slow down the deterioration or even improve the attention of the older adults.

The main contribution of this work is the development of a novel serious game that features parameterizable design settings and incorporation of psychological tests in the game contents. We have also conducted experiments to demonstrate that such a game-based learning system can effectively improve the attention of the older adults.

C. Vaz de Carvalho et al. (Eds.): SGAMES 2015, LNICST 161, pp. 50–57, 2016.
DOI: 10.1007/978-3-319-29060-7_9

2 Related Work

There have been many research efforts invested on the development of simulation games for military training. The Dismounted Soldier Training System is one of the examples. In 2007, Marks [5] evaluated these games from the aspects of editing, content, and gameplay and designed a game for several popular game engines to test their performance in these three aspects. In this work, we have chosen the Unity 3D game engine by the Unity Technologies as our platform for its features of cross-platform and portability to mobile devices. According to Siriarya [6], the older adults are more likely to feel anxious with 3D games due to the unfamiliarity of interactions in a 3D environment. Therefore, in our system, we have chosen to design a 2D game on a tablet computer to avoid complex scenes and interactions.

There have been many researches concerning the changes of cognitive abilities through training. For example, Berry [1] has pointed out that through the training of programming, the functions of working memory of the participants can be improved. Through an affective speech interface, mental disorder can also be effectively improved [4]. Fan et al. [3] combined three types of networks: alerting, orienting, and executive attentions to form the Attention Network Test (ANT), which is also the test that we have adopted for the measurements of attentions in pretest and posttest.

Some researchers have investigated how older adults perceive 3C products (such as personal computer, smart phone and tablet computer) by means of surveys. However, we have not seen much work on incorporating psychological tests to develop games for learning. Caste [2] had conducted a study that used commercial games to train selective attention. However, in order to reduce the effort for designing a new game stage and prevent the users from losing interests on playing the same content repeatedly, it is desirable to have a game that is not only designed specifically for attention training but also be customizable by parameter settings, which is also the design goal of this work.

3 System Design

Most of the commercialized games in the market nowadays target the young or the adults. There are very few games or interface designed specifically for the older adults. Considering the psychological and physiological status of the elderly, the interface design of the game system should be adjusted accordingly. For example, in the user interface, we do not only enlarge all fonts used in all stages, but also have a tips button in game to remind the participants their objectives. In addition, the game system is also designed with appropriate sound effects to strengthen the objectives of the story in each stage. The complexity of the operations demanded in playing game as well as the visual complexity of the interface should also be reduced.

In addition to the consideration of complexity, our game system also includes the following features. First, the proposed system creates game stages on the fly through an external xml file describing tests in a stage, game scenes and other settings. From a user-specified folder, it loads settings such as object type, model name, position, rotation, scale, and other additional script files and creates a game accordingly. In addition, all images or training contents can also be customized through external files. For visual search, the variations of object features such color, shape, size, and status (static/dynamic) can be specified to create variety of games for attention training. Furthermore, our system records all activities in a game session and export the data for further exploration. The recorded data include stage code, stage module, answer, reaction time and object names (target, non-target and distractor).

3.1 System Architecture

The design goal of the game system is to provide a game environment with an intuitive interface and flexible content parameterization for attention training. In order to provide an intuitive interface for the older adults, we aim to design the game for a tablet computer, which has been shown to be more friendly for older adults. The architecture of the system is shown in Fig. 1. Besides the pretests and posttests, the core of game system consists of three components that take inputs of system settings, scene settings and attention training settings. According to these settings, the game system generate a variety of game stages automatically on Unity 3D. The scene settings are the specification of game stages such as stories, dialogues, decorations and triggers. The settings for attention training control the training contexts including training type, number of training objects and object positions in a scene. The process and performance of a user in a game session are recorded for future analysis. With these settings, our system can generate new game stages on the fly without changing the code while providing rich game contents for strengthening training effect. In other words, the users of our game system who have learned markup language (xml) before could create a new game stage easily and quickly by modifying the settings and resources such as stage background image, target-item(image), non-target item, distractor item, story scenario (including text and audio file) and related resources.

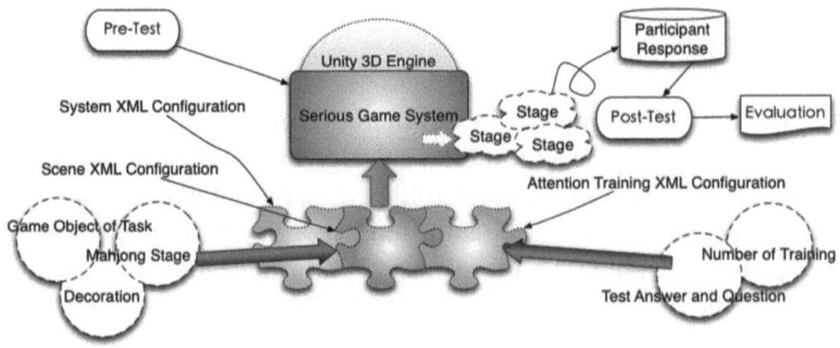

Fig. 1. System architecture of our serious game

3.2 Game Flow

In each stage of our game, a user goes through several steps. The game starts with an introduction screen and a menu for selecting game scenarios. Once a game scenario is selected, the story for the scenario is presented to the user. We have designed the story

Fig. 2. Snapshot of the story mode in a game stage

scenarios to be as common in the daily life of an older adult as possible in order to quickly engage the participants. The system describes the objective of the game and what the participants should focus on during the game. In each stage of the game, the participants are asked to achieve the game objective while obtaining their attention training repeatedly. Each participant is asked to try four different levels (easy, normal, hard, and challenging) of attention training in each stage with six rounds in each level. As depicted in Fig. 2, in each round, there are 15 object items of three types (target, non-target, and distractor) on the screen. The participants are asked to touch the target object under the distraction of the distractor objects which look salient and different from the target object. The target object remains the same in a game scenario while the non-target objects become more and more similar to the target object when the game level become higher. When a game is finished, the participants enter a score page showing their scores, times, and ranks for providing feedback of achievement and motivation for further game playing.

4 Experimental Results

All the participants recruited were randomly assigned to the experimental or control groups with the proportion of about 3:1. The data collected were compared between these two groups to reveal the effects of training with our serious game. Twenty three participants were willing to attend this experiment to have 5-day training. Five of them were male. The range of their age was 69–92, with the mean of 83. Short Portable Mental Status Questionnaire (SPMSQ) was adopted as the screening test for excluding the participants with dementia. None of the participants was excluded.

At the beginning, we have 17 participants in experimental group and 6 participants in control group. But two of the participants in the control group did not complete the experiment. As a result, we have only 4 participants in the control group in the end. Therefore, the data collected from the control group is shown in descriptive statistics for reference only and did not apply a statistical test to compare with that of the experimental group.

4.1 Experimental Design

The whole experiment lasted for three and four weeks for the control group and experimental group, respectively. In the first week, all of the participants were given the pretests (including VS and ANT) individually. In the second week, participants in the experimental group were asked to use the game system for 30 min each day for 5 consecutive days. In each day, the training took place from 3 pm to 5 pm regularly. Participants took the training in batches with 7–9 participants in a batch. The participants in the control group were given other activities using the same device. In the third week, all the participants were given the posttests (also including VS and ANT) individually. Finally, in the fourth week, participants in the experimental group were given a questionnaire asking some questions about the experience or opinions regarding this game system.

The procedure of the whole experiment is as follows: (1) SPMSQ: a screening test to exclude the participants having dementia. (2) Pretest: including 80 trials of the VS task and 96 trials of the ANT task. (3) Training: 30-minute attention training with serious game each day using a tablet computer for the experimental group; 30-minute jigsaw puzzle playing each day using a tablet computer for the control group. (4) Posttest: the same as the pretest. (5) Questionnaire: asking the participants in experimental group some questions about this experiment and game system.

4.2 Experimental Results

4.2.1 Visual Search

In the visual search task, distractors were present or absent with equal probability. The mean accuracy of the 2(distractor: present, absent) × 2(test: pretest, posttest) conditions from the experimental group is shown in Table 1. From the data, we can find that performance of the participants in the posttest is improved compared to the pretest. A two-way ANOVA with repeated-measures applying to this data shows a significant main effect of the test (pretest *vs.* posttest), $F(1,16) = 11.398$, $MSe = 0.293$, $p < .01$. The interaction of distractor and test is not significant. This means that performance improved in the posttest irrespective of the presence or absence of the distractors.

As for the reaction time, variability of the data is rather large. There were large differences even among the participants with the similar age. Although there were also small improvements in the posttest compared to the pretest, the difference between them does not reach significant level statistically. Therefore, the major improvement is shown in accuracy rather than reaction time.

Table 1. Mean accuracy of visual search in pretest and posttest of experimental group.

Distractor	Pretest		Posttest	
Present	0.38	(0.13)	0.51	(0.11)
Absent	0.40	(0.14)	0.52	(0.08)

Note: The value inside the parentheses is standard deviation (SD) of that condition. Accuracy is scored in probability (0-1)

Table 2. Mean accuracy of visual search in pretest and posttest of control group.

Distractor	Pretest		Posttest	
Present	0.41	(0.11)	0.58	(0.01)
absent	0.47	(0.05)	0.54	(0.12)

Note: The value inside the parentheses is SD. Accuracy is scored in probability (0-1)

The accuracy data from the control group is shown in Table 2. There are similar trend as found in the experimental group. But the difference cannot be evidenced by statistical test.

Based on the results of the visual search task discussed above, participants in the experimental group improved their attention in the accuracy data. The training effect of our game system is supported in this respect.

4.2.2 Attention Network Test

Scores of alerting effect, orienting effect and executive control effect are calculated based on the work of Fan et al. [4]. Table 3 shows the mean score of each measure in the pretest and posttest from the experimental group. Mean reaction time and mean accuracy are also included. In these measures, alerting scores reflect the efficiency of achieving and maintaining an alert state. Orienting scores reflect the efficiency of selecting information from sensory input. Scores of executive control reflect the efficiency of resolving conflict among responses.

Table 3. Mean scores of various measures in ANT of experimental group.

	Pretest		Posttest	
Alerting	−0.06	(0.19)	0.04	(0.14)
Orienting	−0.07	(0.17)	0.01	(0.15)
Executive	0.11	(0.17)	0.28	(0.43)
Reaction time	1.82	(0.61)	1.58	(0.44)
Accuracy	0.86	(0.18)	0.98	(0.03)

Note: The value inside the parentheses is SD. Reaction time is measured in seconds. Accuracy is scored in probability

For comparing the scores of pretest and posttest in experimental group, a matched-sample *t* test was applied to each measure separately. The results show that the differences between pretest and posttest in alerting score and orienting score are significant, $t(16) = -1.72, p = .05$; $t(16) = -1.70, p = .05$. In addition, the differences in reaction time and accuracy are also significant, $t(16) = 2.44, p = .01$; $t(16) = -2.81, p = .01$.

Table 4 shows the data from the control group. We found that the mean scores did not differ much between pretest and posttest in most of the measures. Especially, it is worthy to note that alerting score and orienting score improved significantly from the pretest to the posttest in experimental group. However, the same improvement cannot be found in the control group. Overall, the results in ANT show that attention training with our game system can improve the efficiency of alerting network and orienting network. But the effect on executive control network cannot be evidenced.

The improvement of performance in ANT after training is also reflected in the reaction time and accuracy for the experimental group as shown above. This result differs from the result of VS in which the reaction time did not improve after training. It may be due to the high difficulty of VS for the older adults as shown in low accuracy and long reaction time, so that attention training with our game system cannot improve both the accuracy and reaction time in VS.

Table 4. Mean scores of various measures in ANT of control group.

	Pretest		Posttest	
Alerting	−0.13	(0.09)	−0.13	(0.23)
Orienting	−0.19	(0.30)	−0.10	(0.17)
Executive	0.19	(0.10)	−0.06	(0.35)
Reaction time	2.03	(0.64)	1.71	(0.85)
Accuracy	0.84	(0.27)	0.87	(0.23)

Note: The value inside the parentheses is SD. Reaction time is measured in seconds. Accuracy is scored in probability

4.2.3 Analysis of the Data in the Game Process

The data recorded in the process of 5-day training with our game system was analyzed. Among the 17 participants, ten of them improved their reaction time for the color task day by day gradually. Seven participants improved their performance for the color task or shape task abruptly in the second day, and then maintain the same level or improved slowly for the rest of days. In one of the participants, the reaction time for the shape task slowed down gradually.

Furthermore, we divide the participants into the light-using group (n = 8) and heavy-using group (n = 9) based on their total frequency of game-playing in five days. Mean frequency of using in light-using group is 416, with the range of 251–504. Mean frequency of using in heavy-using group is 712, with the range of 507–1179. In the light-using group, only 4 of the 8 participants improved their performance obviously. In contrast, all of the 9 participants in the heavy-using group improved their performance obviously. This result supports the effect of attention training with our game system further.

In order to understand the relationship between frequency of using and the improvement in the attention task (such as ANT), the Pearson product-moment correlation coefficient (r) is calculated. The results show that frequency of using correlated significantly with accuracy in ANT, $r = .551$, $t\,(15) = 2.55$, $p < .05$ (one-tailed). This result echoes the training effect observed in accuracy data discussed above.

5 Conclusions and Future Work

Based on the results of the experiment in this research, playing a serious game incorporating the concept of attention training from cognitive psychology can successfully improve attention in the older adults. Among the three scores in ANT, our game system has effects mostly on the alerting network and orienting network. It means that the older adults can achieve or maintain an alerting state more easily after training. Also they can shift their attention to the critical location with the aid of cue in the environment. All these are important for the older adults in everyday life.

Another contribution of our work is the parameterization in the designing of game for attention training. With parameterization, the adaptability of our game system is increased, and the design cost is reduced. In addition, recording data during the process of game-playing for exploring the learning effect in depth is also available in this approach. Furthermore, we have got mostly positive feedbacks from the participants, demonstrating the effectiveness of our system in engaging the elders in playing the game while getting trainings.

In the future, the degree of customization and parameterization in system design can be augmented further. Presently, the elements under our control include game stage, background story, image, and the test content. In the future, an authoring interface may be designed to provide a more intuitive interaction for creating game stages and test contents. Even more, adjusting the sound effects and particle effects directly through a parameter file is expected to be realized in the new design.

References

1. Berry, A.S., Zanto, T.P., Clapp, W.C., Hardy, J.L., Delahunt, P.B., Mahncke, H.W., Gazzaley, A.: The influence of perceptual training on working memory in older adults. PLoS ONE **5**(7), 11537 (2010)
2. Castel, A.D., Pratt, J., Drummond, E.: The effects of action video game experience on the time course of inhibition of return and the efficiency of visual search. Acta Psychol. **119**(2), 217–230 (2005)
3. Fan, J., McCandliss, B.D., Sommer, T., Raz, A., Posner, M.I.: Testing the efficiency and independence of attentional networks. J. Cogn. Neurosci. **14**(3), 340–347 (2002)
4. Kostoulas, T., Mporas, I., Kocsis, O., Ganchev, T., Katsaounos, N., Santamaría, J., Jiménez-Murcia, S., Fernández-Aranda, F., Fakotakis, N.: Affective speech interface in serious games for supporting therapy of mental disorders. Expert Syst. Appl. **39**(12), 11072–11079 (2012)
5. Marks, S., Windsor, J., Wünsche, B.: Evaluation of game engines for simulated surgical training. In: Proceedings of the 5th International Conference on Computer Graphics and Interactive Techniques in Australia and Southeast Asia, pp. 273–280. ACM, Perth, Australia (2007)
6. Siriaraya, P., Siang, C.: Ang, age differences in the perception of social presence in the use of 3D virtual world for social interaction. Interact. Comput. **24**(4), 280–291 (2012)
7. Slegers, K., van Boxtel, M.P.J., Jolles, J.: Computer use in older adults: determinants and the relationship with cognitive change over a 6 year episode. Comput. Hum. Behav. **28**(1), 1–10 (2012)

Sensitizing: Helping Children Design Serious Games for a Surrogate Population

Gavin Sim(✉), Matthew Horton, and Janet C. Read

ChiCI Group, University of Central Lancashire, Preston, UK
{grsim,mplhorton,jcread}@uclan.ac.uk

Abstract. This paper describes a study to investigate to what extent the use of sensitizing techniques can help children design a serious game for a surrogate population. In total 25 children from a UK primary school aged between 8–9 participated in two design sessions. The first session was designed to inform the children about life in rural China. The second session briefly taught the children about aspects of food hygiene and then required them to design a game on this subject, for children in rural China. The outputs from the children were analysed and although all the children managed to design a game, only 6 related this at all to food hygiene, with three of these having only a single element of food hygiene present. The other 19 created games were unrelated to food hygiene. In addition, only 1 drawing showed any evidence of thinking about the target users. More work is required to understand what children can contribute to the general development of serious games and to the specifics of thinking about other populations.

Keywords: Children · Serious games · Sensitizing · Participatory design

1 Introduction

Serious games are designed with an emphasis on learning [1], as opposed to being purely for entertainment [2]. The effectiveness of serious games to enhance learning in contexts where traditional learning has been found to have limited success, for instance in health [3], has been widely recognized. When the target audience of the games are children research has highlighted the importance of including children in the design process to maximize the potential success of a product.

In terms of design, many studies have shown that participatory approaches with children both at the ideation stage and at the pre-build stage, can be beneficial, although there are concerns about the extent of, and the abilities associated with, children's participation [4].

At root, participatory design is a form of collaborative working, by which groups of users can influence design decisions. Participatory design sessions are generally used to capture design ideas in which the participants are the target user group, for example children designing interactive games for museums [5]. Typical participatory design sessions involve end-users working with designers to propose and work through potential design ideas for a specific system. There are different models of running participatory design sessions in which design experts (software designers and researchers) work with

C. Vaz de Carvalho et al. (Eds.): SGAMES 2015, LNICST 161, pp. 58–65, 2016.
DOI: 10.1007/978-3-319-29060-7_10

domain experts (the end-users, children) to produce designs. It is acknowledged that depending on the way in which participatory sessions are set up, end-users' ideas will have varying impact on the final design. When participants contribute directly to a design, as in a facilitated, as opposed to an informant role, it is especially important that they understand the nature of the artefact they are contributing to, and are aware of why and how they are contributing [6].

The games industry is a global business; with games being developed for a global audience and serious games are situated within this business model. Merritt and Stolterman argue that attention to culture is critical in today's global digital economy but this has been absent from participatory design approaches [7]. Research has been performed to try and improve participatory design practices in developing nations [8]. However, it may not be practical for developers to use participatory design techniques with children from a number of continents, so for this reason, explorations with participatory design for surrogate users may be worth examining.

Children as designers of products for other children is a theme that has been studied [9, 10]. In the first of these two studies, children were actually designing for themselves but were 'informed' that they were designing for another. The use of scenarios that masked the design and the use of practices that diverted the real purpose of the game which was being designed from the participating children had the children believing they were designing for a third party but a third party that was almost identical to themselves. In the second study children were asked to develop a serious game for children in Uganda relating to hand washing. All the children were able to contribute design ideas for a game relating to hand washing but the ideas were mostly aligned to western cultures and artifacts. To overcome this shortcoming sensitization to the culture and beliefs of the target audience may be required.

Sensitization can involve a process in which the participants are encouraged to reflect on past experiences to help facilitate envisioning future experiences. This could be achieved through the use of cultural probes which have been used to gain contextually sensitive information in order to inform and inspire design [11]. Cultural probes are designed objects, or physical packets containing open-ended, provocative and implicit tasks to support engagement with the design process. For example, one of the tasks that children were asked to perform in a study by Wyeth and Diercke [12] was to draw a picture of a classroom of the future and it was found to be effective as a tool to inspire designs. Other methods that have been used to understand the target users include observation, interviews and diary techniques in an attempt to understand the lives of residents in a care home [13].

This paper explores the area of participatory design with children in the UK designing a serious game for children from another culture. The aim of the study presented here was to focus on the design aspects of this experience, by investigating to what extent sensitizing can aid children's designs within participatory design session. Given the poor cultural associations seen in [9], the overarching research question was, would children sensitized to the needs of similar others be better able to design a serious game for that group.

2 Study

The aim of the study was to investigate to what extent the use of sensitizing techniques could aid children to design a serious game for children in rural China. The study firstly required sensitizing children to how life in China differed from their own lives and then a follow on design session in which the children would design a serious game for that population.

2.1 Participants

The participants were 25 school children from a UK primary school; the children were aged 7–8 years old. The children took part in this study within their own school.

As outlined above, there were two separate sessions and two researchers and the teachers were present for both, with an additional researcher being present for the design session only. All the researchers had experience of running participatory design sessions with children and had also worked with the children on other projects so were familiar to them. Teachers and researchers were on hand to encourage the children in their work, but were careful not to influence their design ideas.

2.2 Procedure

The first session aimed to introduce the children to the culture and life in rural China. This took place one week before the second session, which was the design activity. The children had already been learning about China in school and had been reading in class the book 'Secret Agent Jack Stalwart The Puzzle of the Missing Panda: China' as part of their studies [14]. Thus the sensitizing session aimed to build on their existing knowledge, focusing on children in rural China and considering how their lives were similar to and different from those of UK children.

Each child completed activities to elicit information about their existing knowledge and to then explore further life in rural China. There were four activities, which were:

- Knowledge: Write three things already known about China.
- Imagination: Describe a child's Saturday in rural China. This was broken down into three sections; morning, afternoon and evening.
- Learning: After seeing some videos of life in rural China, and a brief discussion of the content of the videos. The children were provided with a set of three pages of images in a montage consisting of images of people and life in rural China. They were required to produce a storyboard using these images telling of a day in rural China. For this activity children were given an A1 piece of paper and worked in groups of either two or three. An example can be seen in Fig. 1.
- Reflection: Write down three things they had learnt from the session.

The second session took place one week after the first session. The aim of this session was to have the children design a serious game to teach children in rural China about food hygiene. This subject was judged to be suitable for the children, as they had covered some of this subject in school but additionally it was relevant to them and to children in

Fig. 1. Example of a storyboard created by the children about the day in the life

rural China. The session began with the children gathered around a white board for a 15 min interactive discussion about aspects of food safety including, preparation, cooking and storage. The children contributed to the discussion by sharing their understanding of the subject, whilst the researcher captured these points on the white board and discussed other points. Once this initial discussion about food safety was completed, the children had the design activity explained to them including details about the future possible use of their designs [4]. The children were given a booklet made up of three blank interfaces for them to complete. The children were asked to create a game for children in rural China teaching them about food safety. They were informed to design their game based upon the knowledge from the previous week and from the information on the white board; they were given their own storyboards from session 1 activity 3 to look at for ideas. Some of the children opted to work in pairs although the majority worked individually. During this process the researchers went round the tables asking the children about their design and encouraging them if they were having problems.

2.3 Analysis

Analysing children's drawings is an established method within child computer interaction [15]. A set of criteria to measure to what extent the participants understood the culture of the target users were applied for the purpose of this analysis of drawings. These criteria were initially based upon the definition of culture proposed by Porter and Samovar [16]:

- Culturally Situated: These designs were firmly grounded in the designer's own culture, requiring understanding of this culture in order to understand and interpret the design unambiguously.
- Culturally Un-situated: These designs assumed no understanding related to the participants' own culture, explaining or including instructions for any element in the design that may be unfamiliar to the target user.

- Experientially Situated: These designs made use of experiences with which the target users was assumed to be familiar based upon the information in the first design session and their work in class.

The drawings were also analysed to determine whether the game was related to the topic of food hygiene and also as to whether any of the knowledge gained from the sensitizing session had been incorporated into the designs.

3 Results

After the end of session 1 the children were asked to state 3 things they had learnt about China; these are displayed in Table 1 below.

Table 1. The things children claim to have learnt after the sensitizing session

Learnt	Number of children
Have long & dangerous journey to school	15
Eat different foods	7
Slept at school	2
Eat on floor	1
Help on farm	6
Poor school facilities	3
Collect water	1
Different religion	1
Use chop sticks	1

In the second session 25 game designs were created, these varied considerably in detail and quality. At one extreme a child simply described a game offering no visuals and at another level some children presented visuals, discussed the interaction and included the game mechanics.

Of the 25 designs 19 did not relate at all to the topic of food hygiene. Of these 19 games, the types of game varied considerably with 5 relating to healthy eating, 3 being platform style games in which food was collected and 4 considering making food but not covering the hygiene aspects of food preparation. Table 2 shows the style of game for all 25 games designed by the children.

Three of the games evidenced a single aspect of food hygiene by including hand washing. In addition three games were reasonably aligned to the scenario. Two of these games involved storing food in the correct location and position. For example, the meat had to go at the bottom of the fridge. Another game involved food preparation with different chopping boards and the user had to select the correct board for the item and ensure the food was washed.

The cultural dimension was analysed for the 25 drawings and the results are shown in Table 3 for the 3 criteria.

As can be seen from Table 3, the majority of the designs were culturally un-situated. The number in brackets indicates that a small element of this category was present in a

Table 2. The types of games depicted in the children's drawings.

Game style	Number of drawings
Healthy eating	5
Hiding food	2
Word search	2
Jumping game	3
Building toys	1
Making food	6
Fishing	2
Washing hands	1
Storing food	2

drawing, for example one storyboard had Chinese characters on the first screen but was still largely culturally un-situated. There was no evidence of any of the children applying the knowledge (see Table 1) from the first session to their games. The games designed were largely culturally neutral. For example one of the games was a platform game that you had to run along, jumping onto different platforms and collecting chickens, this was judged to be culturally un-situated (although it did not relate to food hygiene).

Table 3. The number of children's drawings matching the cultural criteria.

Criteria	Number of drawings
Culturally situated	8
Culturally un-situated	17 (2)
Experientially situated	(1)

4 Discussion

Developing a serious game is complex which is probably why so many frameworks have been developed to aid this process [17]. For children to be successful at designing a serious game they would need to be able to design learning, game mechanics, understand the technology and, in this instance or for any global market, design culturally appropriate content into a game. This may be challenging for children and require more support than was provided in this study.

In this study the children could not describe a serious game solution for the context, which contrasts with the earlier work described in [10, 18] in which the children successfully designed a game relating to hand washing. It may have been that the subject of food hygiene was too complex or too broad for the children to turn into a game. The children might have required more help with ideation prior to creating their games. This could be through the process of playing examples of serious games and enhancing the material that was presented to the children.

In summary, although sensitizing techniques were used prior to the game design session in an attempt to enhance the children's understanding of the target audience of the game, the resulting game designs did not recognize these cultural influences. Of the

25 designs only 1 depicted anything relating to China. Some of the drawings were clearly culturally situated having western influences including pizza, fish and chips and certain household furniture but most of the games were culturally neutral so would have been suitable for the target audience. In order to make the games more experientially situated more material, or more focus might have been needed.

Extending the duration in which the children are exposed to cultural information may help further their understanding of the cultural beliefs of the target population. More varied activities may be required incorporating online material, discussions and videos to enhance their understanding.

5 Conclusion

It is clear from the data within the study that children could propose ideas for a game but in this instance the majority of the games proposed were not related to the scenario of food hygiene and were not experientially situated.

It was anticipated that sensitizing would help children understand the culture of the target user and design a game for them. It was evident from the drawings the children came up with, that this was not the case, with many of the games appearing to show western content or were generic games that are culturally un-situated. The design of culturally un-situated games may not necessarily be a problem as the ideas may be generic enough to be playable to a global audience. It is clear that there are many dimensions that are required to develop a game and children do appear to understand some of these dimensions. More work is clearly required to understand what techniques would help facilitate children design a serious game and the relationship between time and the dimensions.

References

1. Stone, R.: Serious games. Defence Manag. J. **31**, 142–144 (2005)
2. Gee, J.P.: What Video Games Have to Teach Us About Learning. Palgrave MacMillan, New York (2007)
3. Kato, P.M.: Video games in health care: closing the gap. Rev. Gen. Psychol. **14**, 113–121 (2010)
4. Read, J.C., Gregory, P., MacFarlane, S.J., McManus, B., Gray, P., Patel, R.: An investigation of participatory design with children - informant, balanced and facilitated design. In: Interaction Design and Children, pp. 53–64. Shaker Publishing (2002)
5. Dindler, C., Iversen, O.S., Smith, R., Veerasawmy, R.: Participatory design at the museum: inquiring into children's everyday engagement in cultural heritage. In: OZCHI, pp. 72–79. ACM, Brisbane (2010)
6. Read, J.C., Fitton, D., Horton, M.: Giving ideas an equal chance: inclusion and representation in participatory design with children. In: Proceedings of the 2014 Conference on Interaction Design and Children, pp. 105–114. ACM, Aarhus (2014)
7. Merritt, S., Stolterman, E.: Cultural hybridity in participatory design. In: Proceedings of the 12th Participatory Design Conference: Exploratory Papers, Workshop Descriptions, Industry Cases, vol. 2, pp. 73–76. ACM, (2012)

8. Dearden, A., Rizvi, H.: Adapting participatory and agile software methods to participatory rural development. In: Proceedings of the Tenth Anniversary Conference on Participatory Design 2008, pp. 221–225. Indiana University (2008)
9. Mazzone, E., Read, J.C., Beale, R.: Design with and for disaffected teenagers. In: 5th Nordi Conference on Human-Computer Interaction: Building Bridges, vol. 358, pp. 290–297. ACM, Lund (2008)
10. Read, J.C., Sim, G., Gregory, P., Xu, D.Y., Ode, J.-B.: Children Designing Serious Games. EAI Endorsed Trans. Serious Games 1 (2013)
11. Gaver, W., Dunne, A.: Projected realities: conceptual design for cultural effect. In: Proceedings of the SIGCHI Conference on Human Factors in Computing Systems, pp. 600–607. ACM, Pittsburgh (1999)
12. Wyeth, P., Diercke, C.: Designing cultural probes for children. In: Proceedings of the 18th Australia conference on Computer-Human Interaction: Design: Activities, Artefacts and Environments, pp. 385–388. ACM, Sydney (2006)
13. Müller, C., Neufeldt, C., Randall, D., Wulf, V.: ICT-development in residential care settings: sensitizing design to the life circumstances of the residents of a care home. In: Proceedings of the SIGCHI Conference on Human Factors in Computing Systems, pp. 2639–2648. ACM, Austin (2012)
14. Hunt, E.S.: Secret Agent Jack Stalwart: The Puzzle of teh Missing Panda: China. Weinstein Books, New York (2008)
15. Xu, Y., Read, J.C., Sim, G., McManus, B., Qualter, P.: Children and smart technologies: can children's experiences be interpreted and coded. HCI 2009 People and Computers, pp. 224–231. British Computer Society, Cambridge (2009)
16. Porter, R.E., Samovar, L.A.: An introduction to intercultural communication. In: Samovar, L.A., Porter, R.A. (eds.) Intercultural Communication: A Reader, pp. 4–26. Wadsworth, Belmont (1994)
17. de Freitas, S., Jarvis, S.: A framework for developing serious games to meet learner needs. Interservice? Industry Training, Simulation and Education Conference, Orlando, FL (2006)
18. Sim, G., Read, J.C., Gregory, P., Xu, D.: From England to Uganda: children designing and evaluating serious games. Hum.-Comput. Interact. **30**, 263–293 (2014)

Chess Playing and Mathematics: An Exploratory Study in the South African Context

Luneta Kakoma[1,2] and Apostolos (Paul) Giannakopoulos[1,2(✉)]

[1] University of Johannesburg, Johannesburg, South Africa
kluneta@uj.ac.za, gianna@unisa.ac.za
[2] University of South Africa, Pretoria, South Africa

Abstract. In 2014 the University of Johannesburg undertook a study into the role that chess plays in the learning of Mathematics. According to authors' knowledge, it is one of the biggest studies undertaken which involved 10 teachers and about 1800 learners. The study although it was predominantly exploratory, it is also to some extent confirmatory as it involved also some control schools as well as comparative as it also involved an Ugandan school. The uniqueness of the South African situation which lies between a First World and a Third World country offers some new insights into the role that chess plays in the teaching and learning of mathematics. Preliminary results show that there is a correlation between playing chess and the learning of Mathematics.

Keywords: Mathematics · Foundation phase · Chess · Transfer · Critical thinking · Problem solving

1 Introduction

The use of games in general and use of chess in particular in the teaching-learning situation is not something new. Back in the 60s a psychologist, Adrian de Groot [1] became very interested in the use of chess as an educational tool. He observed particularly that there was a significant different approach between the 'experts' (grand masters)' and the new to the game, the 'novices'. He assumed that the latter under the guidance of the former they will also become experts.

In the early 80's Foundation (ACF) introduced chess in schools in order to improve the mathematical skills of the learners through critical thinking and problem solving skills which are evident in a chess player. In South Africa the MiniChess programme (MCP) [2] was introduced in some disadvantaged primary schools in Grades R to 3, having the backing of the Russian Grandmaster Gary Kasparov. In South Africa alone it has trained more than 1300 teachers since 2008 and it is active in more than 170 schools [2].

The University of Johannesburg in collaboration with MCP undertook to investigate the effects of chess on Mathematics for Grades R-3. This paper reports on this study that took place in 2014 and was a predominantly exploratory and partially confirmatory. The results will form the basis for the next phase, the intervention phase in 2015.

C. Vaz de Carvalho et al. (Eds.): SGAMES 2015, LNICST 161, pp. 66–73, 2016.
DOI: 10.1007/978-3-319-29060-7_11

2 Literature Review

The role of playing games in order to enhance teaching and learning has been researched for more than 50 years. The results have been inconclusive [3–5]. There can be many reasons for it and the most important one could be the problem of transfer. Although a lot of research [3, 6] has been done on transfer it still remains an elusive concept. There is no single definition of transfer as it depends on the context. For example, transfer within a domain or in different domains [6], transfer of knowledge and skills [5], transfer of training [7] ability to generalize, or transfer of knowledge to solve problems in novel situations [8]. Failure by the learner to see the analogy or the novelty of the new situation, leads to unsuccessful transfer of his/her existing knowledge [9]. For Billing [6], problem-solving, learning and transfer are similar cognitive activities.

Gobat and Campitelli [3] pose the question that most experts on transfer have posed in general: "Can a set of skills acquired in a specific domain (in our case chess) generalize to other domains (e.g., mathematics, reading) or to general abilities (e.g. reasoning, memory)?" There is no agreement between researchers if that is possible or not. This study is not trying to answer this question directly but it is based on evidence that chess can enhance various cognitive abilities.

Billing [6] conducted an extensive research on transfer where he surveyed 700 analytical and evaluative papers with good empirical evidence to back up any claim where the tasks were of high cognitive content. His conclusions could be summed up by Alexander and Murphy [10] (cited in [6]). These authors state that educators should take cognisance of one of the generalisations on transfer that ...transfer of knowledge and procedures learned through instruction occurs far less often than educators hope; and that there are three components involved in transfer: the learner, the content and the context. These two important findings also form part of the essence of this study.

2.1 Chess and Mathematics

As it was stated earlier de Groot [1] was one of the first to see the importance of chess as an educational tool and others [3, 10, 11]. Research by Christiaen [12], Fried and Ginsburg [11] and others [5, 13] found that learners receiving instruction in chess had gained an academic advantage over the control group not receiving instruction in chess, even cognitive, perceptual-motor, and emotional gains. At the center of chess playing is thinking, intuitive and conscious, and training children to think from an early stage can only improve their cognitive abilities [13].

In the '80s it was the ACF embarked on the Chess in Schools programme as it was established then that learners that engage in chess regularly their maths scores improved by about 18 %. Research done by a number of authors [13–15] came to regard chess as a model for cognitive processes and abilities such as perception, information management, attention, memory, logical thinking and problem solving. Playing chess also involves a combination of aptitudes, such as analysis, logical and critical thinking. It means that ability in chess is not due to the only one or two abilities of individuals but due to a large number of aptitudes that work together [5, 13].

According to Feldhusen et al. [16] they also highlighted a number of benefits of studying and playing chess, not just for gifted children: it raises intelligence quotient (IQ) scores, strengthens problem solving skills, teaching how to make difficult and abstract decisions independently; enhance reading, memory, language, and mathematical abilities.

Gaudreau [17] further showed the value of chess for developing problem-solving skills also among young children. Using "Challenging Mathematics", the average problem solving score of students increased from 62 % to 81 %. Another study by Liptrap [5] and others [13, 18] also showed that chess can improve both reading scores and mathematics for elementary students.

Another view is that learning chess develops some sort of informal handling of mathematical concepts which might be better than formal learning [18]. In the framework of Barrett and Fish [13], without knowledge about the concept of joint probability, chess-playing children excellently performed in calibration tests.

However other studies conducted proved that, the benefits of chess in learning in general and mathematics in particular is questioned. Most of the studies based their argument on the claim that chess masters had the ability to store innumerable configurations and the best moves associated with each in long-term memory rather than having developed superior problem solving skills [4, 18]. This argument though could be true for grown up players and not for children at Foundation phase where playing any form of game does carry educational value. The only question is 'To what extent?".

Based on the benefits that chess has in the learning of Mathematics in South Africa the MiniChess Association [2] brought chess playing to some disadvantaged primary schools as an additional form of enhancing the learning of Mathematics. In order to evaluate the effects of chess on the teaching and learning of Mathematics at Foundation levels the following research was conducted.

3 Research Methodology

The study was a predominantly exploratory quantitative quasi-experimental study. Since it involved 10 primary schools and 1800 learners and it was the first of its kind in South Africa of such a great scale, it was decided by the researchers to divide it into three phases. In 2014 Phase I is reported here. Phase II for 2015 will be the interventionist phase and Phase III in 2017 the evaluation phase.

It was also decided that 4 schools could be used as control schools (See Table 1, No 7-No10) in order to get a preliminary idea about chess playing schools and non-chess playing schools. These schools' Grades wrote the test of the previous Grade. For example Grade 1, wrote the standarised test of Grade R. Grade 2 wrote the standarised test of Grade 1 and so on. Furthermore, since MiniChess [2] it was used for a comparative study. For anonymity sake schools were numbered as No 1- No 10. The experimental schools had 1 h of chess every week. At the end of the course all schools wrote standarised tests supplied by the South African Department of Basic Education (DBE) [19] where copies of the tests can be obtained.

Table 1. Standarised tests results per school

Schools	N	R	N	Gr1	N	Gr2	N	Gr3
No 1	74	67	60	65	63	59	62	46
No 2	69	78	75	71	36	29	81	31
No 3	39	72	40	70	46	64	48	35
No 4	56	64	65	65	24	56	45	38
No 5			43	29	20	30	45	19
No 6	27	47	43	46	20	29	24	6
Ave (excl 6)		70		60		46		34
No 7	77	72	64	57	60	46		
No 8	64	61	54	50	57	46		
No 9			147	53				
No 10	64	63	59	61	58	50		
Aver.		65.3		55.3		47.3		
Totals	470		650		384		305	

The study being predominantly exploratory as stated earlier, as it tried to establish the competency of the learners in the various sections of mathematics it also worked on the hypothesis that chess can have a positive effect on the learning of mathematics, as a result control (non-chess playing schools) and experimental groups were also used.

The Method. None of the 10 schools used had chess in their schools before. The Mini-Chess Association provided trainers who trained the teachers in the use of chess for educational purposes. The course comprises of 4 levels one for each Grade (R-3) In most of the cases mathematics is ‘camouflaged’, as it is implicitly involved as well as various cognitive functions like, decision making, logic, anticipating and so on.

In school No 9 only Grade 1 participated in the experiment while in school No 5 Grade R did not participate and school No 6 is the Ugandan school. From the control schools, in school No 8 only Grade 1 test was written. The tests comprised of 57 items for Grade R, 97 items for Grade 1, 107 items for Grade 2 and 97 items for Grade 3. In addition to the tests interviews were conducted with the teachers from the six schools that participated in chess.

The Results. In Table 1 the results from the standardised tests appear with N the number of learners in each grade and school and the other columns represent the average marks for all Grade R- Grade 3 for each school (No1–No10) as some schools had more than one class in a certain grade. For example, school’s No1 all Grade R learners obtained an average of 67 % while for school No 6 all Grade 1 learners obtained an average of 46 %. The averages of the experimental and control schools is also shown where for the experimental group were 70 % (Gr R), 60 % (Gr 1), 48 % (Gr 2) (excluding the Ugandan school) and the corresponding averages for Grades R-2, 65.3 %, 55.3 % and 47 % respectively. The total number of number of learners that participated was 1809.

4 Analysis of Results and Performance on Various Mathematical Concepts - Summary

Since this study was predominantly exploratory and many schools were involved it was decided to look for trends first and then look for important points that explain the effects if any in the teaching and learning of Mathematics if chess is used as a way to enhance various cognitive abilities. Performances between the schools were not analysed as that was not part of the research aim.

- For both experimental and control groups there is a decline on the average performance from Grade R to Grade 3. This means that as the learners were advancing in their grades their knowledge of mathematics was declining.
- The highest correlation between experimental and control groups occurs in Grade 3 where the averages are the lowest for both groups
- The lowest correlation occurs in Grade 2 where the experimental schools performed slightly worse than the control groups.
- The Ugandan school performed worse than all schools.
- Where the number of learners was low (less than 45) these schools performed better. This means that the less the number of learners in class the better their performance in Mathematics.
- Having used t-tests for the experimental and control groups the calculated values of t were −1 08, −0.57 and 25.30 for Grades R, 1 and 2 respectively. These were significant at $p > 0.2$, $p > 0.2$ and $p > 0.00$ levels.

All school underperformed in Grade R.(less than 40 %) on a number of questions especially those that required providing an explanation. On average less than 40 % was achieved in all the grades from 1 to 3. This points to an alarming picture about mathematics in the country. This study concurs with other studies that have established that learners' mathematical knowledge is very weak in all grades.

For Grade R the concepts that were identified as problematic were: writing numbers correctly, vocabulary, shape recognition, telling time. For Grade 1, shape recognition is still a problem as well as time telling. In addition to these, describing fractions of shapes using mathematical symbols, problems with, $>$, $<$, $\geq$, and $\leq$, and data handling and graphing were problematic.

In Grade 2, some learners can still not write the numbers from 1–100, or identify what the next number is, estimation, time telling, equality and inequality and place value which creates problems with arithmetic operations. Data handling is still problematic as well as sequencing days of the week and matching shapes with their corresponding names.

Finally for Grade 3, estimation, place value, long multiplication, difficulty in using comparative words such as 'more than', 'less than', symmetry, and more than 65 % could not name polygons.

4.1 Analysis of Teachers' Interviews

Teachers from the 6 experimental schools were interviewed at the end of the year, and below is a summary of what they said.

- The teachers all agreed that learners loved MiniChess and were very enthusiastic and motivated about it;
- The teachers have noticed that learners seem to have improved in their attention span as they stay quiet longer tan before;
- The teachers admitted that the learners social skills have improved;
- Almost all the teachers agreed that they do not see the link between chess and the curriculum;
- The teachers suggested that MiniChess must be part of the school curricula;
- The majority of the teacher confessed that they still cannot play chess and relied on the facilitators to instruct the learners.

5 Discussion and Future Directions

The study produced some encouraging results. This was due to the fact that there is sufficient ground to accept the hypothesis that chess playing enhances problem solving skills and concept formation. Huge problems were encountered with sequencing, pattern recognition, matching words and shapes or shapes that share same attributes (square and rectangle) contrasting them to other shapes (i.e. circles). Fractions (numerical and two dimensional shapes) also posed problems.

A number of uncontrolled variables could also have contributed to less than expected performance:

(a) The teachers
  - The training of teachers, how they use chess and incorporate it to mathematics.
  - Teachers themselves are not conversant with chess.
  - It is possible teachers treated chess as a game for recreational purposes.

(b) The trainers of the teachers
  - The training of teachers was not monitored by the researchers. As a result it is possible that the training of the teachers could have been flawed.
  - The trainers themselves were not educationalists.

(c) Other factors
  - The Principals of the schools allowed only one afternoon a week for chess. Perhaps after school the children were too tired too.
  - The length of the standarised tests could have been a bit long as in some schools they could only finish 80 % of the test.

In order to move to the second phase, the intervention phase, it is necessary firstly to collect more data from teachers and learners through interviews and focus group interviews. Then analyse in more detail all concepts that many learners have a problem with and design interventions to improve learning. Teachers will receive particular training to teach such concepts rather than reaping the benefits of playing chess indirectly.

For example existing chess materials will be directly connected to mathematics. Then in the midyear learners could be retested and the results will be processed. At the end of the year based on the findings, new mathematics materials can be developed which connect more chess playing and problem solving.

The following year the process will be repeated and finally materials can be developed to be part of the school curriculum. In Grade R and Grade 1 it might be a good idea to translate the English concepts to some vernacular to remove the problem of language as a barrier to learning since Foundation phase learners are taught mostly in their vernacular. The research team agreed that it is almost impossible to conclude from the learners' one year engagement with MiniChess that it had a definite bearing on their mathematical growth. The research team will:

- Investigate the cognitive development of the learners over a period of two years.
- Develop mathematics questions that attend to problem-solving, critical and strategic thinking
- Investigate the learners' growth in mathematical competence over the period of two years.
- Develop learners and teachers' support materials that link chess to the mathematics curricula and give appropriate training..

6 Conclusion

Introducing chess at an early stage of a child's development could have positive effects in the teaching and learning of mathematics especially in a developing country. However for it to succeed it is absolutely necessary to train primary school teachers as to how to use chess as a supplementary tool to enhance various cognitive functions (and there is evidence to that effect) but also using chess as a game for recreation, numeracy, two dimensional thinking, logic and viewing mathematics critically.

Acknowledgements. We thank Tsongo Sun and Moves for Life and Minichess for financing this project and supplying the MiniChess materials and trainers.

References

1. De Groot, A.D.: Thought and Choice in Chess. Mouton, The Hague (1965)
2. MiniChess Programme. http://www.minichess.co.za/. Accessed 10 December 2014
3. Gobet, F., Campitelli, G.: Educational Benefits of Chess Instruction: A Critical Review. http://www.brunel.ac.uk/~hsstffg/preprints/chess_and_education.PDF. Accessed 20 January 2015
4. Sweller, J., Clark, R.E., Kirchner, P.A.: Why minimal guidance during instruction does not work: an analysis of the failure of the constructivist, discovery, problem-based, experiential, and inquiry based teaching. Educ. Psychol. **41**, 75–86 (2006)
5. Liptrap, J.M.: Chess and standard test scores. Chess Life **53**(3), 41–43 (1998)
6. Billing, D.: Teaching for transfer of core/key skills in higher education: cognitive skills. High. Educ. **53**, 483–516 (2007)

7. Hesketh, B.: Dilemmas in training for transfer and retention. Appl. Psychol. Int. Rev. **46**(4), 317–386 (1997, 1999)
8. Sorensen, R.: Effective Teaching in High School. Sage Publications, London (2003)
9. Kaminski, J.A., Sloutsky, V.M., Heckler, A.: Transfer of mathematical knowledge: the portability of generic instantiations. Child Dev. Perspect. **3**(3), 51–155 (2009)
10. Alexander, P.A., Murphy, P.K.: Nurturing the seeds of transfer: a domain specific perspective. Int. J. Educ. Res. **31**(7), 561–576 (1999)
11. Fried, N., Ginsburg, N.: (n.d). The Effect of Playing Chess on Cognitive, Perceptual and Emotional Development in Children. http://www.usechess.org/scholastic/sc-research.html. Accessed 23 January 2015
12. Christiaen, J.: Chess and cognitive development. Unpublished Master's thesis. Gent, Belgium (1976)
13. Barrett, D.C., Fish, W.W.: Our move: using chess to improve mathematics achievement for students who receive special education services. Int. J. Spec. Educ. **26**(3), 181–193 (2011)
14. Buki, J., Ho, F.: The Effect of Math and Chess Integrated Instruction on Math Scores | PRLog. The Chess Academy, Chicago. http://www.prlog.org/10086633-the-effect-of-math-and-chess-integrated-instruction-on-math-scores.html. Accessed 23 January 2015
15. Campitelli, G., Gobet, F.: The role of practice in chess: a longitudinal study. Learn. Individ. Differ. **18**, 446–458 (2008)
16. Feldhusen, J.F., Rifner, P.J.: Checkmate: capturing gifted students' logical thinking using chess. Gifted Child Today Mag. **20**(1), 36–39 (1997)
17. Gaudreau, L.: A Study Comparing the Challenging Mathematics Curriculum to Traditional Math. http://www.scholasticchess.mb.ca/docs/ciers.pdf. Accessed 10 December 2014
18. Romano, B.: Does Playing Chess Improve Learning? Promising (Inexpensive) Results from Italy (2011)
19. South African Department of Education (DBE). http://www.education.gov.za/Curriculum/AnnualNationalAssessment/tabid/424/Default.aspx. Accessed 20 January 2014

A Virtual City Environment for Engineering Problem Based Learning

Olivier Heidmann[1,2(✉)], Carlos Vaz De Carvalho[1,2], Hariklia Tsalapatas[1,2], Rene Alimisi[1,2], and Elias Houstis[1,2]

[1] University of Thessaly, Argonafton and Filellinon, 38221 Volos, Greece
[2] Institute for Research and Technology Thessaly, Demetriados 95 and Pavlou Mela, 38333 Volos, Greece
olivier.heidmann@gmail.com, carlosvazcarvalho@gmail.com, htsalapa@inf.uth.gr, ralimisi@gmail.com, enh@gmail.com

Abstract. Secondary education students often struggle with Mathematics and Science, preventing them to follow a successful career in Engineering. At a higher education level, problems still exist, including in their motivation levels. A Problem-Based Learning approach can offer an interesting solution to help circumvent this issue by creating an environment in which the learners themselves seek out information and create strategies to solve the training situation. This present work, named project eCity, aims at creating a Virtual Learning Environment platform in the form of a city building simulator, in which students, often digital native, will feel at ease and encouraged to solve the practical engineering scenarios they will face. The eCity platform targets at the same time students from the secondary education and students from higher education, allowing them to work together in a close relation to solve the presented problems together.

Keywords: Engineering · Problem-based learning · Virtual environment · Serious games · Communities

1 Introduction

The difficulty that secondary education students have with Mathematics and other Science disciplines is a widespread problem in Europe as stated by several international comparative studies like PISA or TIMMS. This prevents these students from following a technical academic path like Engineering. And even when they do so, they still face a lot of problems on these disciplines at Higher Education level and become demotivated. This is not due to lesser skills of these students but mostly due to wrong educational strategies. We cannot forget that this generation is the "net-generation" or "digital natives": they are used to technology, they absorb information in shorter chunks, they expect instant responses and feedback, they want interactive and immersive forms of learning and they want to be active in their learning.

Problem-based learning (PBL) is a learner-centered pedagogy in which students are assessed on their ability to go through a problem solving process, usually based on real-life situations. In a convergent path, games and simulations can be instantiated for learning as they involve mental and physical stimulation and develop practical skills – they force the

C. Vaz de Carvalho et al. (Eds.): SGAMES 2015, LNICST 161, pp. 74–79, 2016.
DOI: 10.1007/978-3-319-29060-7_12

player to decide, to choose, to define priorities, to solve problems, etc. Games can also be social environments, sometimes involving large distributed communities. They imply self-learning abilities (players are often required to seek out information to master the game itself), allow transfer of learning from other realities and are inherently experiential with the engagement of multiple senses. Therefore, gaming and simulation environments are excellent learning tools because, through Virtual Environments, they can replicate real contexts or even provide training situations that occur in very specific circumstances while retaining the players' motivation to learn. Mixing PBL, games, simulations and virtual environments provides a Virtual Learning Environment (VLE) where digital natives feel comfortable because they are immersed in technology, they can communicate and they are active.

Engineering is one of the areas where PBL is a valid learning alternative/complement to the traditional methods. An engineer is a professional practitioner, concerned with applying scientific knowledge and innovation to develop solutions for technical problems. The work of engineers forms the link between scientific discoveries and their subsequent applications to human needs through new technological solutions. The responsibilities of the engineer may include defining problems, conducting and narrowing research, analyzing criteria, finding and analyzing solutions, and making decisions. Engineers must weigh different design choices on their merits and choose the solution that best matches the requirements. Their crucial and unique task is to identify, understand, and interpret the constraints on a design in order to produce a successful result.

Authors such as Woods [1] and Lacuesta et al. [2] confirmed in their studies the benefits of PBL for engineering students – considerable improvements in critical, lateral and creative thinking, problem solving strategies, intrinsic motivation, group collaboration, communication skills, entrepreneurship and collaboration with society and regional development. According to Kolmos [3] President of the European Society for Engineering Education, the implementation of innovative learning methods such as PBL in engineering education may be regarded as "the higher engineering education's response strategy to requirements from society". From an engineering perspective, the interdisciplinary perspective that PBL proposes plays an important role since most innovation and real-life problem solving is based on cross disciplinary, interdisciplinary and collaborative knowledge.

The objective of the eCity project is to design a PBL-based educational platform, based on an open-source city-building simulator/game (SimCity like) and explore its simulation engine to support city development problems that relate to math, science and engineering concepts. This platform will be used for two different purposes: to motivate secondary students to an engineering academic path and to scaffold learning for higher education engineering students. This will happen simultaneously as students from both education levels will form heterogeneous groups where the older students can guide the younger ones in the finding of the correct solution.

The development and expansion of the (virtual) city will be accomplished through the involvement of the platform users, with the availability of problems and challenges with different levels of complexity. The challenges and problems listed in the (virtual) city are based on real life situations and the learners' solutions exploited in the resolution or improvement of those situations can then be based on their experience from the real world. For example, students must design an energy efficient school campus or develop plans for a sewage system. Therefore the virtual city can be considered as a graphical representation of the infinite number of problems that arise every day, in real-life, giving the learners a closer touch with their future professional responsibilities. Furthermore, they will be able to address problems collaboratively, working with colleagues from other European countries, namely Portugal, Spain, Italy, Greece and Turkey.

2 A Virtual City Environment to Foster Interest in Engineering

The eCity virtual environment [4], available on the eCity portal [5] is designed as a PBL-oriented, online, collaborative VLE platform, based on a city-development simulation engine that stimulates the integration and continuous exploitation of Problem Based Learning. The platform will be used collaboratively by students from secondary and vocational schools and higher education engineering schools.

ECity's PBL VLE is expected to be a general and stimulating context especially due to the nature and complexity of the range of problems that will be available in the virtual city. The platform will also promote a sense of belonging to a community, peer support and an additional rewarding system that includes reputation points for problem solving allowing the establishment of rankings (promoting an healthy competition); the "immortality" of the learner's work – his/her contribution stays registered and can be accessed by all the users from the game beginnings, stimulating once more the recognition motivation mechanism (Fig. 1).

Fig. 1. The eCity portal

Also important is the fact that the platform will be integrated in a clear pedagogical methodology, PBL-oriented, to ensure that the upmost relevance is given to the learning process, not the technology. Problems or challenges can be fed into the platform as homework, teamwork, curricular activities, extra-curricular competitions, big or small projects, etc. PBL can be incorporated within existing structures with little disruption as it can be implemented in a variety of forms. Therefore it is not necessary to change the curricular organization as problems can be formatted to different time and work schemes (Fig. 2).

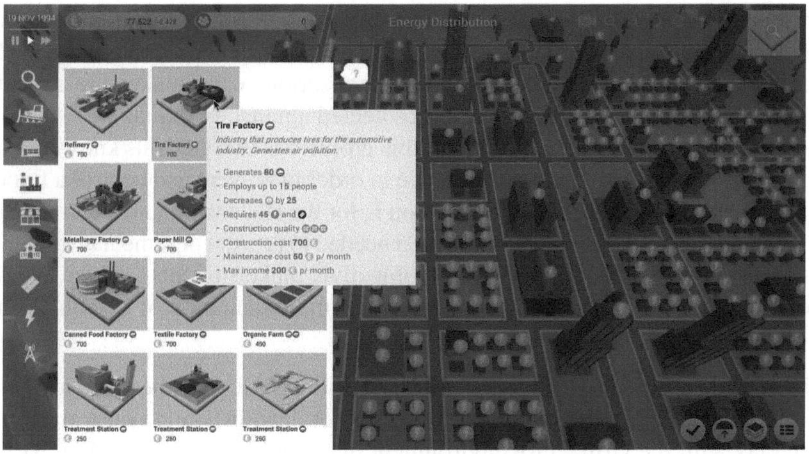

Fig. 2. The eCity virtual learning environment

3 The eCity Project Outcomes

As concrete results, the eCity project will produce several outputs. The first on is an online, collaborative, supporting simulation platform based on the engine of a city-development simulator. This PBL environment is designed to allow an easy transfer of learning from and to other realities due to the enjoyable, dynamic play that replicates real contexts and provides practical training for very specific situations. It is freely available during and after the project for other engineering institutions and secondary schools.

A set of 8 ready-available problems, platform setups and pedagogical guides for free use has also been created. These problems are configurable and customizable, for instance to reflect real situations in the partners cities. They address the following issues:

- Energy Distribution. The objective of this scenario is to learn and understand basic knowledge about energy distribution. There are different types of voltages used for the electrical current, and the one needed for a domestic usage is not the same than the one needed in a factory, which itself might differ from the one produced by a power plant.
- Renewable Energy. This scenario aims to motivate the students in the problem of energy supply in general and to familiarize them with the renewable energies as alternative methods to produce energy.
- Internet Connection Coverage (ISP). The main objective of this scenario is that students know and understand basics of data distribution networks. They could achieve some basic concepts of the ISPs (Internet Service Providers) and data distribution while they are playing.
- Mobile Phone Coverage. This game is introduced as an initial contact with the basics of the design of mobile network (MN), and students will be able to deploy different elements, only antennas to simplify, that make up a mobile network on a map of a given city.

- Earthquake Protection. This scenario focuses on creating a city that is protected against earthquakes and on raising awareness about earthquake protection, itself part of curriculum in countries like Turkey, where serious earthquakes are expected to occur but most of the buildings are not protected against earthquakes.
- Flood Protection. The main objective of this problem is that students know and understand the basic actions to be put in practice in order to prevent and control a flood.
- Pollution. The main objective of this lesson is for the students to know and understand basic notions about pollution and the action needed to prevent or remediate to pollution.
- Bus Network. This scenario has a main objective: make students analyze and design an optimal graph structure, represented by the implementation of a public transportation network.

In addition to those scenarios, all users will also be allowed to play the game in a sandbox mode. In this situation there is no given goal or set deadlines and constraints and the user can play with the virtual city environment in a totally free fashion (Fig. 3).

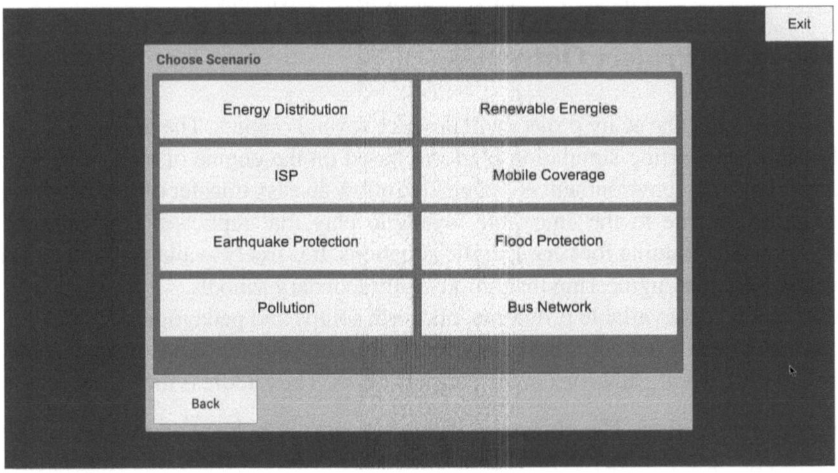

Fig. 3. The 8 engineering problems currently available in the eCity VLE

The project also produces a validated pedagogical methodology to integrate the eCity platform that can be replicated in other engineering schools. In fact this methodology is composed by two different complementary approaches:

- On one side, it will be the engineering students themselves that will develop new challenges and problems. This way they will be directly applying the concepts learned at higher education.
- On the other side, they will be solving the set of project-developed challenges plus the new ones with the support of secondary/vocational students. By doing this they will scaffold their engineering learning but will develop other skills like leadership, group work and collaboration.

Finally, the project shapes a motivational methodology, to be used in secondary and vocational schools to integrate the eCity platform as a complementary activity for students to develop their interest and motivation towards engineering.

4 Conclusions

The eCity PBL-based EVL and the accompanying methodology have been designed with the objective of contributing to help students in the secondary and higher education level with engineering-related courses and issues, and to foster their desire to successfully pursue an Engineering-related career.

The software and all related activities are currently under deployment in real-life contexts in secondary schools and Universities in Greece, Portugal, Spain, Italy and Turkey. In the project scope it will be possible to directly reach about a thousand individuals from the different countries involved, shared between teachers, high school students and university students.

Early results demonstrate so far a positive impact on the engagement of students and high degree of motivation thanks to the engaging and captivating software.

Acknowledgements. This work is funded with support from the European Commission, Life Long Learning Programme. The publication reflects the views of the authors only and the Commission cannot be held responsible for any use made of the information within.

References

1. Woods, D.R.: Helping your students gain the most from PBL (2000). http://elc.fhda.edu/transformReno/resources/Woods-2000.pdf
2. Lacuesta, R., Palacios, G., Fernandez, L.: Active learning through problem based learning methodology in engineering education. In: 39th Frontiers in Education, San Antonio (2009)
3. Anette Kolomos, coordinator for the EU project, Socrates project, PBL-Engineering which has developed the master program: Problem Based Learning in Engineering and Science
4. eCity portal. http://ecity-project.eu/
5. eCity VLE. http://ecity-project.eu/en/game/

Knowledge Improvement of Dental Students in Thailand and UK Through an Online Serious Game in Dental Public Health

Kawin Sipiyaruk[1,2(✉)], Stylianos Hatzipanagos[3], Jennifer E. Gallagher[1], and Patricia A. Reynolds[1]

[1] Dental Institute, King's College London, London, UK
{kawin.sipiyaruk,jenny.gallagher,p.a.reynolds}@kcl.ac.uk
[2] Faculty of Dentistry, Mahidol University, Phutthamonthon, Thailand
[3] Centre for Technology Enhanced Learning, King's College London, London, UK
s.hatzipanagos@kcl.ac.uk

Abstract. A serious game for Dental Public Health (DPH), GRAPHIC, was developed to support students in designing health promotion programmes at King's College London. Based on the evaluation data from an initial pilot study, there was evidence that GRAPHIC had the potential to be a global learning tool. Taking this evidence into account, a new version of GRAPHIC in Thai language was developed for students at Mahidol University in Thailand. King's and Mahidol dental students piloted these two otherwise identical versions in January and February 2015 to test the knowledge acquisition in DPH. The students were given the opportunity to carry out activities in GRAPHIC, including completing pre- and post-knowledge tests. The initial findings support the effectiveness of GRAPHIC as a learning tool because the disciplinary knowledge of students from both institutions was significantly improved after interacting with the game. The paper presents these findings and makes recommendations for further improvements to the game.

Keywords: Dental education · Dental public health · Educational game · Online learning · Serious game

1 Introduction

Computer based gaming has been applied to government, military, education, and healthcare sectors, where related applications come under the term 'serious games' [1]. Serious games can provide new teaching and learning environments, which can engage students [2, 3]. In the context of Dental Public Health (DPH), which is defined as "the science and art of preventing oral disease, promoting oral health and the quality of life through the organized efforts and informed choices of the society, organisations, public and private, communities and individuals" [4], it would be very helpful for learners to experience authentic situations where they must make decisions about the suitable oral health promotion programmes in a simulated environment.

C. Vaz de Carvalho et al. (Eds.): SGAMES 2015, LNICST 161, pp. 80–85, 2016.
DOI: 10.1007/978-3-319-29060-7_13

GRAPHIC (Games Research Applied to Public Health with Innovative Collaboration), a serious web-based game for DPH, was developed to support students in designing health promotion programmes for a given population at King's College London. Based on the data from an earlier pilot study at Mahidol University, in Thailand, the design of GRAPHIC was considered suitable for use as a global learning tool in Europe and Asia [5, 6]. The evaluation identified some required modifications, most notably translation of the content into the Thai language. Therefore, a new version of GRAPHIC in the Thai language was developed to pilot test GRAPHIC in Thailand.

This study aimed to investigate the feasibility of using GRAPHIC for DPH knowledge improvement in the UK and Thailand as part of a wider study evaluating the impact of serious games as learning tools, ultimately supporting students in different learning cultures. The paper therefore presents the evaluation of the knowledge improvement of the multilingual pilot version of GRAPHIC by assessing students' knowledge acquisition through using GRAPHIC in UK and Thailand.

2 Methods

To achieve the objective, we engaged a quantitative methodology approach to collect research data. The following sections provide a description of the methods we employed.

2.1 GRAPHIC Design

GRAPHIC was developed as a web-based application, built with Java Enterprise technologies and was deployed on a secure cloud server, where dental students can access the game using a web browser, such as Internet Explorer, Safari, Chrome, etc. Within GRAPHIC, the students were expected to learn several topics in DPH, which included common risk factors, the Ottawa Charter, and the Dahlgren and Whitehead model. To achieve this, students were firstly given information about the context of the game: i.e. that as game participants they would be operating in a simulated town, where they would be exposed to influencing factors in a real life context from provided demographic data of a virtual community. After that, they needed to complete the game by making decisions regarding the suitability of oral health programmes in simulated situations and selecting the best five recommended options of the programmes in order to improve the oral health of the population in the community of the game. The latest version of GRAPHIC has a revised game engine, learning design, and content (e.g. learning scenario) that has been modified to suit students in both countries of this investigation. The modifications were based on the findings of previous studies of GRAPHIC, including taking serious game theories and the outcome of related research into account. The game also has been developed to include English and Thai versions. King's and Mahidol dental students piloted this latest version of GRAPHIC in January and February 2015 respectively to assess the acquisition of knowledge in DPH as part of a wider feasibility and impact study of the game (Fig. 1).

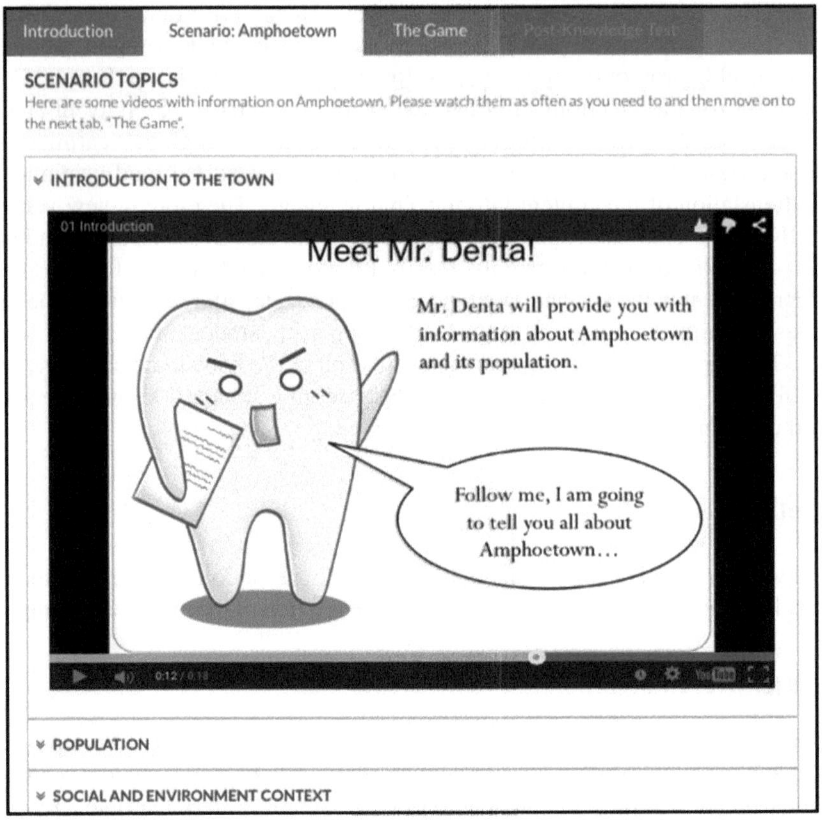

Fig. 1. A screen capture of GRAPHIC where information of a learning scenario is provided

2.2 Participants

Undergraduate dental students with similar levels of achievement in the dental curricula of UK and Thailand were assigned to complete GRAPHIC as a mandatory activity. All students who were eligible to use GRAPHIC must have used the game as a requirement of the courses, but they could decide whether to participate in this study by submitting a consent form. Unique identifiers were used in order to identify students to participate in the study.

2.3 Data Collection

The students from both institutions were given similar guidance about the process and the same preparatory information including a video on YouTube. However, the set-up could not be identical, as there was a limitation due to insufficient space of Mahidol computer room. The process was that the students from both institutions were asked to complete a pre-knowledge test in order to assess their pre-knowledge. After that, they had to complete the game by submitting the best five oral health promotion interventions. Finally, they were asked to complete a post-knowledge test in order to assess their post-knowledge after interacting with the game. They were all given unlimited attempts of answer submissions to complete the game but were required to submit the pre- and post- knowledge tests in one attempt. The tests consisted of 20 questions relating to the learning outcomes, which were validated by the King's tutors with an agreement from the Mahidol tutors. The questions were similar, but question sequencing was different between the pre- and post-tests. The students were also asked to complete a feasibility questionnaire voluntarily. The tests were automatically recorded as part of the quiz function of the game, and the results made available through spreadsheets downloaded from the analytics capability of the gaming engine. The scores of the pre- and post-tests were compared using paired *t*-test in each country in order to evaluate the knowledge improvement after interacting with the game. In addition, differences of the pre- and post-test scores were compared between two countries using independent *t*-test in order to assess whether there were differences in the knowledge of the students between institutions.

2.4 Ethical Considerations

Ethical Approval had previously been obtained from Biomedical Sciences, Dentistry, Medicine and Natural & Mathematical Sciences Research Ethics Subcommittee (BDM RESC), King's College London (KCL) College Research Ethics Committees (CREC), application number BDM/13/14-117 on 15th July 2014 and Faculty of Dentistry and from Faculty of Pharmacy, Mahidol University, Institutional Review Board (MU-DT/PY-IRB), application number MU-DT/PY-IRB 2015/002 on 19th January 2015.

3 Findings

There were 82 King's and 92 Mahidol students who decided to participate in the feasibility study and completed the game including the pre- and post-tests. This represents 55.41 % of the UK and 80.7 % of the Thai student groups that were targeted.

According to Table 1, for the King's students, the mean of pre-test score was 14.87 (SD = 3.05) and the mean of post-test score was 16.06 (SD = 2.98). The post-test score was significantly higher than the pre-test score ($t = -3.841$, $p \leq 0.001$). Similarly, for the Mahidol students, the mean of pre-test score was 14.49 (SD = 3.55) and the mean of post-test score was 15.23 (SD = 3.24). The post-test score was significantly higher than the pre-test score ($t = -2.036$, $p \leq 0.05$). The data suggest that the knowledge of the students from both institutions was significantly improved after interaction with GRAPHIC.

According to Table 2, there were no significant differences in pre-test score, post-test score, and score difference between both institutions. The findings suggested that the students from both institutions had broadly similar level of pre-knowledge and knowledge improvement.

Table 1. Pre- and post-test scores

Samples	Pre-test score		Post-test score		*t*-value
	Mean	SD	Mean	SD	
King's	14.87	3.05	16.06	2.98	−3.841***
Mahidol	14.49	3.55	15.23	3.24	−2.036*

Note: *Significant at $p \leq 0.05$; ***Significant at $p \leq 0.001$.

Table 2. Comparison of test score between two institutions

Scores	King's		Mahidol		*t*-value
	Mean	SD	Mean	SD	
Pre-test score	14.87	3.05	14.49	3.55	0.746
Post-test score	16.06	2.98	15.23	3.24	1.756
Score difference	1.2	2.82	0.74	3.48	0.942

4 Discussion

The findings support the educational value of GRAPHIC as a global learning tool (a tool which, because of its particular design and content knowledge, has an impact on learners, coming from two different locations and cultures), in UK and Thailand, as the knowledge of students from both institutions was improved after interacting with the game, which supports the effectiveness of GRAPHIC. Another aspect that should be taken into consideration is that students in different learning cultures tend to have different attitudes towards their learning, e.g. Asian students may not be familiar with self-directed learning [7], and GRAPHIC is a self-directed learning tool, where students are able to complete the game on their own time and place. However, the findings suggest that students' performance from both countries was not significantly different when using GRAPHIC, although their learning cultures were different. It could be argued that, as digital natives, students from both countries were familiar with technologies, especially video games. In addition, there was an induction, introductory video where students can learn how to navigate the game. These may be able to facilitate students' use of the game.

Based on the initial findings of this feasibility study, the running of GRAPHIC in both institutions was shown to be feasible. Although it is the first time that all final year Mahidol dental students used GRAPHIC, there appeared to be no issues with access and use in Thailand, supporting the use of GRAPHIC half way across the world would work. However, knowledge improvement alone is not enough to evaluate the game quality, but there should also be further evaluation of usability, including how many attempts learners use to complete the game, how students navigate through the game, and how the game engages the students.

5 Conclusion

Overall, this study demonstrates that both UK and Thai students have improved their DPH knowledge in playing GRAPHIC. Therefore, a serious game like GRAPHIC can be used for DPH courses in both institutions. An enhanced version of GRAPHIC will be developed to be used in the academic year 2015/16 and it will take these findings into account, as part of the wider study. In addition, to enhance the validity of this study, GRAPHIC trial settings in both schools will be further harmonised.

References

1. Zyda, M.: From visual simulation to virtual reality to games. Computer **38**(9), 25–32 (2005)
2. Breuer, J., Bente, G.: Why so serious? On the relation of serious games and learning. Eludamos. J. Comput. Game Cult. **4**(1), 7–24 (2010)
3. Davis, J.S.: Games and students: creating innovative professionals. Am. J. Bus. Educ. **4**(1), 1–11 (2011)
4. Gallagher, J.E.: Wanless: a public health knight. Securing good health for the whole population. Community Dent. Health **22**(2), 66–70 (2005)
5. Sipiyaruk, K., Gallagher, J.E., Hatzipanagos, S., Cornforth, J., Reynolds, P.A.: An evaluation of the analytic data from the GRAPHIC game II (Games Research Applied to Public Health with Innovative Collaboration) played by a cohort of year 5 undergraduate dental students. BULLGIRSO (in press)
6. Sipiyaruk, K., Gallagher, J.E., Hatzipanagos, S., Cornforth, J., Reynolds, P.A.: A global setting for GRAPHIC: an online serious game for dental public health – a pilot study. (Abstract). In: Proceedings, 13th Innovations in Education Colloquium, University of Brescia, Italy, 22–26 April 2015
7. Tweed, R.G., Lehman, D.R.: Learning considered within a cultural context: Confucian and Socratic approaches. Am. Psychol. **57**(2), 89–99 (2002)

A Gamified Community for Fostering Learning Engagement Towards Preventing Early School Leaving

Hariklia Tsalapatas[1,2](✉), Olivier Heidmann[1,2], Rene Alimisi[1,2], Dimitris Koutsaftikis[1,2], Spyros Tsalapatas[1,2], and Elias Houstis[1,2]

[1] University of Thessaly, Argonafton and Filellinon, 38221 Volos, Greece
[2] Institute for Research and Technology Thessaly, Demetriados 95 and Pavlou Mela, 38333 Volos, Greece
htsalapa@uth.gr, olivier.heidmann@gmail.com, ralimisi@gmail.com, dikoutsa@gmail.com, spyros@meliploe.com, enh@gmail.com

Abstract. Early school leaving is a complex phenomenon that may adversely affect on a learner's future development. ESL is the result of a combination of factors, such as insufficient school curricula understanding, low value placed on education by families, unavailability or low capacity of parents to support learners in schooling, insufficient parent-teacher-learner communication, and more. Many factors are socio-economic and are related to the extended social environment of learners. This work aims at strengthening the ties of school networks aiming at preventing ESL risk factors to set root in a learner's life through early interventions that start in primary school. This is pursued through a gamified school community and supporting gamified complementary to school curricula learning activities that aim at fostering engagement of parents, teachers, and learners. The community promotes a sense of affiliation, opens-up communication channels, and promotes a positive school environment for the benefit of learners and their parents.

Keywords: Communities · Gamification · Inclusion · Early school leaving

1 Introduction

Early school leaving (ESL) have adverse effects on the future development of a child, personal and professional. ESL leads to the inadequate acquisition of skills and as a result may inhibit the fulfillment of a child's full potential [1]. This can be a result of access to reduced professional opportunities as a consequence of limited skill sets which, in turn, results to higher unemployment risk and higher risk of social exclusion and poverty [2]. For this reason, EU countries have renewed objectives initially set in 2010 of reducing ESL rates to less than 10 % by 2020 [3].

ESL has significant negative consequences on the well-being of an individual. According the a study of US graduates 56 % of ESLs are unemployed as compared to 16 % of those who have graduated [4]. Other studies show that ESLs may show social maladjustments such as behavioral disorders and delinquency [5–7].

C. Vaz de Carvalho et al. (Eds.): SGAMES 2015, LNICST 161, pp. 86–93, 2016.
DOI: 10.1007/978-3-319-29060-7_14

The above indicate that addressing ESL is more relevant than ever for the benefit of individuals and communities towards enhancing smart, sustainable, and inclusive growth, individual and community well-being, and social cohesion [3, 8].

Initiatives for addressing ESL can be widely categorized as actions for mitigation and actions for prevention. Mitigation efforts usually focus on bringing individuals that have left school back into the educational system with the objective of completing at least secondary education [9]. Such initiatives include second chance schools, transitional classes and more. Prevention efforts typically strive to identify individuals that are at risk of dropping out of school and subsequently providing a support structure for ensuring that these individuals will continue to be engaged in formal education. Prevention initiatives include after school study, personalized learning paths, and mentor support [9].

According to the ET2020 Working Group on Schools Policy ESL is a complex phenomenon that cannot be 'attributed solely to schools or be solved by schools alone' [10]. There is not one single factor that contributes to ESL. ESL is a complex phenomenon that is a result of a combination of factors that may differ in urban vs. rural areas as well from one cultural and economic environment to another. However, some factors emerge as significant: understanding of school curricula by learners and parents, especially of migrants exposed to a new school and social environment; low value on education placed by families who may consider work at a young age as a viable alternative to education; the socio-economic background of a family, including families of low income or with unemployed parents [11]; low availability of parents to help their children with learning and schooling, for example with homework as a result of lack of skills or long working hours; insufficient communication among parents, teachers, and learners; a perception that school curricula are not tied to or relevant in real life; and more. Research demonstrates a link between parental engagement in a child's learning early on, in ages 3–9, and dropout rates at the age of 17 as evidenced through an analysis of the child-parent center programs in the City of Chicago [12].

The LINC project builds on early work on preventing ESL by focusing on enhancing the engagement of the entire school community, including parents, learners, and teachers with the objective of reinforcing social networks that can support learners to stay in school [13, 14]. The proposed learning interventions start early on, in primary education, and continue throughout lower secondary education. Through this approach the project aims at preventing ESL contributing factors from setting root in a child's life by enhancing communication among learners, parents, and teachers, building the confidence and potential of parents to effectively contribute in their child's learning and schooling, and empowering teachers to become leaders in their school communities on preventing ESL by enhancing their capacity to design community-building activities. The above are pursued through two main activities: the development of a gamified school community that encourages parent participation in school life and opens-up channels of communication among parents and teachers and the introduction of gamified learning activities designed for joined execution between parents and learners the results of which are made available through the LINC virtual community.

The proposed ESL preventing community is validated through real-life learning pilots that take place in Greece, Sweden, France, and the Czech Republic. Early results demonstrate positive reactions of parents and teachers and a sense of affiliation and community. The work will be completed in November 2015.

2 A Virtual School Community for Preventing ESL

The LINC virtual community [15] is designed as a complementary tool that can be exploited for enhancing community-building activities that already take place in schools. The objective of the community is to strengthen the ties of the social network of teachers, parents, and learners in a particular school or network of schools and to contribute to the development of a positive, enabling, and supporting environment for learners, parents, and teachers with the objective of preventing ESL contributing factors to become ESL risks [14].

For parents, the community introduces a set of resources that allow them to develop awareness of ESL contributing factors, to build understanding of school curricula, and to be informed on events and activities in which they can participate for promoting their own lifelong skill development with the objective of enabling them to become meaningfully engaged in their child's schooling and learning. In addition, the community provides services through which parents can communicate with each other as well as directly and easily with their child's teachers proving an additional channel for making school easily accessible. Parents can further review projects of their children with the objective of coming closer to the activities that take place in the classroom. Furthermore, through the community parents can easily communicate with their child's teachers through links to the teachers' professional email accounts provided upon login in a personalized manner to each parent (see Fig. 1, right).

Fig. 1. The LINC virtual community for preventing ESL: individualized login screen (left); home screen for parents with direct communication links to teachers (right).

For teachers, the community offers access to content and links to resources related to building a thorough understanding of the issue of ESL as well as ESL contributing factors. It allows communication with other teachers for the exchange of knowledge and good practices on the issue of ESL. It promotes communication with parents publicly through forums and personally through email. Most importantly, it introduces learning sheets that describe learning activities that can be deployed in the context of school collaboration for enhancing communication among all members of the school community, including parents, learners, and teachers with the objective of helping teachers become leaders in their school communities on initiating activities that help prevent ESL.

For learners, the community offers the possibility to publish school projects either related to the proposed community-building activities or wider classroom practices introducing a sense of achievement and self-confidence. This function further promotes a community spirit among class members. Publication is allowed either with teacher mediation or, for older learners, with parent consent. Safe navigation of the community is achieved through account-controlled access that allows only members of a specific school community to use the services.

Content can be published on the LINC community by community members. Individuals become members of the community after approval to ensure control on who has access to the services; this is an important point for ensuring the protection of learners and for ensuring that community members are related to participating schools. LINC community members can either create articles and publish them as resources or publish with references links to interesting articles related to education, educational and cultural activities that may be of interest to school learners and teachers, events, articles on ESL, and more.

The LINC community is not designed for use as a standalone service. Rather, the community is designed as a complementary educational tool that helps integrate informal and formal learning practices in schools through the active engagement of all school community members, including teachers, learners, and parents [14]. The community allows the monitored publication of outcomes of learning activities and projects that take place either in the context of formal school curricula subjects, such as math, science, or culture, or in the context of extra-curricula activities, as for example visits to museums or engagement with technology beyond school curricula requirements in off-school hours, including weekends.

3 Gamification of Community-Based Learning Activities Designed for Increasing School Ties and Learning Process Engagement

Gamification of learning processes refers to the introduction of gaming elements and mechanics in learning design [17]. This work discusses the introduction of gamification elements in primary and secondary education community building initiatives in the context of LINC.

Gamification elements in the LINC virtual community aim at promoting engagement with the learning process of all school community members in an inclusive manner with the objective of creating a positive and supportive school environment that allows learners, parents, ant teachers to feel affiliated to the school network. This inclusive process that engages not only learners but also parents is part of a wider, holistic learning design that supports learners both in schooling, i.e. in educational activities related to school curricula and the school program, as well as learning, i.e. in wider knowledge and skill building efforts that are part of a learner's everyday life [12]. The community aims at complementing existing school practices by introducing conditions that help further engagement in learning of individuals that can positively affect a learner's educational efforts, including teachers and parents.

More specifically, gamification in LINC promotes communication, fosters participation in learning, and helps build a community spirit of collaboration, competition, and inclusion. Gamification is introduced at three levels:

- In the learning activities themselves, which are organized as learning games
- In the community functionality through rewards and recognition mechanisms
- Through links to social media

Gamification in learning activities is manifested through actual learning activity design. The activities that have been proposed by schools and school teachers that are members of the LINC network are diverse and span the school curriculum.

Many of the proposed learning activities introduce gaming principles such as searching for pieces of information that combined can be used for synthesizing the solution to a puzzle as is the case in the treasure hunt and s-troll activities; competing in terms of reaching a rich solution in the minimum amount of time among participating teams, a design element deployed in the cultural treasure hunt activity; role-playing approaches such as those used in the reversed classroom activity; exploring and collaborating in a group, as deployed in the Arduino programming activity; and more.

Furthermore, the virtual community design integrates gamification elements in informal learning activities in the form of rewards that aim to enhance participation. The following gamification elements are supported:

- A 'participant' component in which photos, profiles, and activities of members can be observed by others in the community. By joining the community a user can immediately see his or her profile in the community group thus getting immediately a sense of affiliation
- A 'hall of fame' component is further presented in the home page of a user upon log in presents photos of the most active users in terms of publishing and reviewing content. By clicking on the photo a user can see the profile of the hall of fame member
- 'Stars' and 'badges' are attributed to users that achieve a specific number of publications to the community or a specific number of article reviews

Additional gamification elements may be implemented into the community functionality in the future through suggestions of community members.

Finally, the LINC community is connected to popular social media such as Facebook® and Twitter®. A LINC community Facebook® page provides an alternative interface for communicating with other members. Users can optionally connect to the LINC services via their Facebook® account if they do not want to create a LINC account. Notably the existence of a Facebook® account is not a requirement for connecting to the LINC community, which attributes to users dedicated LINC accounts upon user request and approval by the LINC administrators, but is only supported by LINC as an alternative log-in process. The information on the LINC Facebook® page is replicated in a corresponding community module that is visible on the home page of each user. Similarly, posts on the forums of the LINC community are replicated on the LINC Facebook® page.

4 Early Piloting of Gamified Community-Based Learning Activities

The LINC community-based learning methodologies [14], the related gamified learning activities [14], and the proof-of-concept virtual community [15] are being validated in practice through deployment in learning experiments that engage learners, parents, and teachers in real-life learning contexts in Greece, France, Sweden, and the Czech Republic. During the evaluation learners and their parents participate under teacher mediation in one or more of the inclusive learning activities described above working in pairs or groups for achieving learning goals and objectives. The activities to be deployed are selected by each participating school based on the interests of the wider school community that surrounds a specific class.

One of the early activities that has been implemented was Arduino programming for exposing learners, parents, and teachers to the magic of technology as a means for synthesizing solutions to given puzzles [14]. As shown below in Fig. 2, learners worked in pairs with their parents. A total of 16 individuals participated voluntarily in the early activities that took place in March 2015. In an introductory session, learners and their parents were exposed for the first time to the Arduino platform and its objective of allowing users to solve problems in a constructivist [16] manner that advocates that knowledge is synthesized rather than transmitted, that learners already possess knowledge on which they build every time the engage in learning, and that the teacher is a facilitator in explorative learning processes. Learners and their parents were presented to basic functionality of the Arduino® platform and the corresponding programming environment that allows interaction with external constructions. Through the programming platform learners and their parents executed simple, introductory exercises such as lighting a led, producing sounds, and more. The efforts of the teams were documented in digital projects that were published through the LINC virtual community for the benefit of the entire participating class and for fostering a sense of achievement and pride in the completion of a non-trivial exercise.

The participants in the learning activities, learners, parents, and teachers, reacted in a very positive manner. Viewing programming as a serious game enabled the highly

Fig. 2. Arduino programming activity with the participation of learners and their parents that work as a team for implementing non-trivial ICT-related activities.

engaged participation of learners and parents in activities that complemented school curricula in science and math. Parents particularly commented in a positive manner on the opportunity to work with their children on projects that they initially considered as complex and were particularly satisfied to achieve completion of the given exercises under the mediation of teachers and engineers that were present for guidance and support. The follow-up to the learning activities that is provided through the publication, under teacher mediation, of projects onto the LINC community further introduced an element of recognition of achievement and acted as a bridge activity between two consecutive Arduino programming sessions. Through the posting of results on the virtual community learners and parents had the opportunity to review their efforts and introduce additional comments, an activity that further enhanced communication among school community members. Finally, teachers commented that the gamified learning activities allowed learners to take initiatives that introduced a sense of ownership of their own learning and schooling activities, allowed them to self-evaluated their existing knowledge and desired learning goals, and promoted a sense of advanced responsibility on their behalf towards enhancing their knowledge for their own benefit. This was demonstrated by requests by learners towards their teachers to provide them with additional activities for further developing related skills.

5 Conclusions

The LINC gamified learning community and learning activities designed for joined execution by learners and parents have been designed with the objective contributing to the preventing of ESL through early and continuous interventions that start in primary school and continue throughout lower high school with the objective of strengthening the ties of the wider school community of learners, parents, and teachers, promoting enhanced communication, building the self-confidence of parents in their ability to effectively engage in the schooling and learning of their children, and introducing good practice paradigms in the form of learning activities designed for fostering engagement in learning processes. The community and related activities are currently under deployment in real-life contexts in primary and secondary schools in Greece, France, Sweden, and the Czech Republic. Early results demonstrate a positive impact on the engagement of parents in schooling and learning through their participation in activities designed for joined execution with their children. Findings further demonstrate that exposing learners to informal learning that is complementary to school curricula can further promote an interest in educational and help learners understand the connections between education and real-life. Finally, findings demonstrate that teachers recognize the need of mobilizing the extended school community towards preventing ESL and have positive reactions to the proposed interventions through gamified learning design.

Acknowledgements. This work is funded with support from the European Commission, Life Long Learning Programme. The publication reflects the views of the authors only and the Commission cannot be held responsible for any use made of the information within.

References

1. Podilano, C., Tabasso, D., Tseng, Y.-P.: A second chance at education for early school leavers (2012). http://ftp.iza.org/dp6769.pdf
2. Heckman, J., Rubinstein, Y.: The importance of noncognitive skills: lessons from the GED Testing program. Am. Econ. Rev. **91**, 145–49 (2001)
3. European 2020 Target Report (2012). http://ec.europa.eu/europe2020/pdf/themes/29_early_school_leaving.pdf
4. Stanard, R.P.: High school graduation rates in the US: implications for the counseling profession. J. Couns. Dev. **81**(2), 217–221 (2003)
5. Fortin, L., Marcotte, D., Potvin, P., Royer, Ã., Joly, J.: Typology of students at risk of dropping out of school: description by personal, family and school factors. Eur. J. Psychol. Educ. **21**(4), 363–383 (2006)
6. Jimerson, S.R., Anderson, G.E., Whipple, A.D.: Winning the battle and losing the war: examining the relation between grade retention and dropping out of high school. Psychol. Sch. **39**(4), 441–457 (2002)
7. Freeney, Y., O'Connel, M.: Psychological, economic and academic predictors of the intention to leave school early among a sample of Irish students, Working Paper, Combat Poverty Agency (2009). ISBN:978-1-905485-92-5
8. European Centre for the Development of Vocational Training (Cedefop): Guiding at risk youth through learning to work: lessons from across Europe (Research paper no. 3). Publication Office of the European Union, Luxemburg (2010)
9. GHK Consulting Ltd.: study on access to education and training, basic skills and early school leavers: final report, DG EAC 38/04, DG EAC, Brussels (2005). http://ec.europa.eu/education/pdf/doc284_en.pdf
10. Work Programme, ET2020 Working Group on Schools Policy. http://ec.europa.eu/education/policy/strategic-framework/expert-groups/documents/schools-work-programme_en.pdf
11. McGarr, J.: Early school leaving: an exploration of the factors contributing to school non-completion, Master's Degree, Dublin Institute of Technology (2010)
12. Temple, J.A., Reynolds, A.J., Miedel, W.T.: Can early intervention prevent high school dropout? Evidence from the Chicago child-parent centers, Institute for Research and Poverty, Discussion paper no. 1180-98 (1998)
13. The LINC project portal. http://linc-project.eu
14. Tsalapatas, H., Alimisi, R., Heidmann, O.: ESL contributing factor analysis and early, continuous methodological interventions for preventing ESL, LINC project report (2014). http://www.linc-project.eu/images/documents/reports/D2.1_LRM_539024-COMENIUS-2013.pdf
15. LINC virtual community. http://community.linc-project.eu/
16. Papert, S.: Mindstorms: Children, Computers, and Powerful Ideas. Basic Books, New York (1980)
17. Wikipedia, Gamification. http://en.wikipedia.org/wiki/Gamification

Serious Computer Games Design for Active Learning in Teacher Education

Jože Rugelj(✉)

Faculty of Education, University of Ljubljana, Kardeljeva pl. 16, 1000 Ljubljana, Slovenia
joze.rugelj@pef.uni-lj.si

Abstract. Active learning is a pedagogical method that focuses the responsibility of learning on learners. They engage in activities, such as reading, writing, discussion, or problem solving that promote analysis, synthesis, and evaluation of class content. Cooperative learning, problem-based learning, and the use of case methods and simulations are some approaches that promote active learning. Serious games design can provide a framework to support confirmation, structured, and guided inquiry. There is a convergence between the core elements of a good serious game design and the characteristics of productive learning. Another link between games and learning is formative feedback as a critical part of any learning effort and a key component in game design that adjusts challenges.

Keywords: Serious games design · Active learning · Learning goals · Teacher education · Information-communication technology · Formative feedback

1 Introduction

Learning in schools is still heavily geared toward the acquisition of content within a teacher-centered model, with instruction too often abstract and decontextualized and thus not suitable for this age of complexity and interconnectedness. This is especially topical for "*digital generations*", born after 1985. They grew up surrounded by digital media, and most of their activities dealing with peer-to-peer communication and knowledge management, in the widest sense, are mediated by these technologies. The changing ways of how members of this generation learn, communicate, and entertain themselves are the primary reasons behind the growing popularity of social computing applications, sociability, and team spirit, engagement and working attitude, multitasking, individualization and personalization, immediacy, and fluency with multiple media types [11, 13]. But these generations are also called "*gamer generations*" as they spend a lot of their time playing computer games. And as there are many connections between games and learning, educators could integrate games into teaching and learning. Game design has a lot to teach us about learning, and contemporary learning theory has something to teach us about designing better games [18]. Marshall McLuhan, famous Canadian philosopher of communication theory, who predicted World wide Web in sixties, when he talked about a "global village", stated: "*Anyone who makes a distinction between games and learning doesn't know the first thing about either.*"

C. Vaz de Carvalho et al. (Eds.): SGAMES 2015, LNICST 161, pp. 94–102, 2016.
DOI: 10.1007/978-3-319-29060-7_15

Games can lead to changes in attitudes, behavior, and skills and that is actually exactly that how *learning* is defined. We need to explain why game-based learning is engaging and effective and when, with whom and under which conditions games can be integrated into learning.

There is a convergence between the core elements of a good game and the characteristics of productive learning [17]. The constructivist problem-based and active learning methods indicate the success of learning in the context of challenging, open-ended problems. Goal-based scenarios have long been viewed as an active primer for situated learning. Correspondingly, in a good game a player is involved in an iterative cycle of goal-based, interactive problem solving. Another link between games and learning is formative feedback - a critical part of any learning effort [16], and also a key component in good game design that adjusts challenges and gives feedback so that different players feel the game is challenging and their effort is paying off. Well-designed games have the potential to support meaningful learning across a variety of content areas and domains. But all games are not good for all learners and for all educational goals!

Gee claimed [4] that the secret of a good game was not its 3D graphics with bright colors and exciting sounds or music, but its underlying architecture where each level is adapted to the outer limits of the player‘s abilities, seeking at every point to be hard enough to be just doable. Cognitive psychologists have long claimed that the best instruction hovers at the boundary of a student‘s competence. And why aren‘t the games used more widely in classrooms if they are so useful for learning?

While time constraints, cost and availability of appropriate games, and a lack of knowledge about their integration into learning are possible reasons for this, the major problem is the lack of good research on games and learning [19]. Compared to other types of instructional systems, there are too few experimental studies examining the range of effects of gaming environments on learning, and a corresponding lack of theory and practice for their design and implementation.

2 Game Based Learning

In modern education there is a need for shift from traditional didactic transmission models of teaching to the learner-oriented active forms of learning whereby the teacher's role changes radically. Instead of transmitting knowledge, teacher prepares the appropriate environment with different challenges and tasks for independent student learning, guides them and gives them adequate feedback. Learning objectives move from the lower taxonomic levels, which are dominated by recalling information or retrieving various data and facts, to higher taxonomic level, where the focus is on the search for, evaluation and use of knowledge in new settings.

Game is a structured or semi-structured context that looks familiar and relevant and where players find goals that they try to achieve by overcoming challenges. When appropriate learning goals are integrated into game activities, the game can become a learning tool that integrates most of the requirements for modern learning [5].

Prensky [12], Gee [4], and Whitton [20] defined game based learning as *a process of learning with the use of digital games*. Students are directed toward a goal, choosing actions and experiencing the consequences of their activities. They make mistakes in a risk-free setting, and through experimentation they learn actively and practice the right way to do things. They can be additionally stimulated by instant feedback and reward of success. Students remain highly engaged in their activities and cognitive processes that can later be transferred from the game environment to real life. Next to the environment, where learning takes place, games usually provide also motivation, which has many effects on students' learning. It can direct activities toward particular goals, lead to increased effort and energy for learning, increase persistence in activities, affect cognitive processes and enhance performance [9]. All these characteristics increase the chance that the desired learning outcomes will be achieved.

Learning is defined as the activity or process of gaining knowledge or skill by studying, practicing, or experiencing something. As we have just stated, playing games can be an efficient way to learn [10, 21, 22]. But what are the key elements of a good serious game?

Gross [6] stated that serious games must have well defined learning goals and have to promote development of important strategies and skills to increase cognitive and intellectual abilities of learners. According to Malone [8] and Garris [3], the elements contributing to educational values of digital games are sensual stimuli, implemented as visual and audio representations of learning material, fantasy (context presented in imaginary setting), challenge (demanding or stimulating situation) and curiosity (desire to know or learn).

These elements must be integrated into the environment with well defined objectives and rules, the context of meaningful learning, appealing story, immediate feedback, a high degree of interactivity, challenges and competition, as well as random elements of surprise. Games can be social environments, sometimes involving large distributed communities. They imply [1] self-learning abilities where players are often required to seek out information to master the game itself, allow transfer of learning from other realities, and are inherently experiential with the engagement of multiple senses.

Van Eck [19] states that games can be effective learning environments not just because they are fun but because they are immersive, require player to make frequent important decisions, have clever goals, adapt to each player individually and involve social network.

Garris [3] argues that in good serious games instructional content is blurred within game characteristics. Students are playing the game and having fun, forgetting about the "learning" part of the experience even though they are constantly presented with new concepts which they have to adapt in order to be successful in game. More detailed overview of the important characteristics of good serious games can be found in the paper by Zapušek and Rugelj [22].

3 Serious Games Design in Teacher Education

Rieber, Smith and Noah [14] stated already in 1989 that there are two distinct applications of games in education: game playing and game designing. Game playing is the traditional approach where one provides ready-made games to students. Game designing assumes that the act of building a game is itself a path to learning, regardless of whether or not the game turns out to be interesting to other people. The idea of "learning by designing" is based on the assumption that active participation in the design and development process is the best way to learn something. This approach has gained increased prominence due to the proliferation of computer-based design and authoring tools.

At the Faculty of Education, University of Ljubljana we started to implement this approach six years ago in the framework of the two-semester course *Application of ICT in education* for future computer science teachers. There have been a lot of different approaches, methods and ideas developed on how to organize the process of designing and developing educational game from the initial idea into to final product. We could not agree completely with any of them so we decided to develop our own method, called 'SADDIE' [15]. In the following years, we have spread the use of this method to several elective courses at our university, to a course at the University of Rijeka, Croatia, and to postgraduate international summer schools on game based learning that took place in Spain, Estonia, Ireland, Bulgaria and Slovenia.

SADDIE is an acronym of six main project phases: Specification, Analysis, Design, Development, Implementation, and Evaluation. SADDIE is an extension of 'ADDIE' instructional design approach that was developed at the Florida State University in the seventies and was used for designing learning materials for American army [2].

3.1 SADDIE - Methodology for Serious Game Design

The main focus of our approach is project based active learning, where students working in small groups are highly motivated in game design and production. They compete against each other, which team will produce the best serious game, what is seemingly the main goal of their activities. But this is actually only a side effect. The two main learning goals of this process are to learn in an efficient way through carefully refined process of active engagement in the game design and production process and to improve the key teachers' competences. They include the ability to determine learning objectives that are in line with the syllabus, the selection of appropriate teaching approaches and their implementation in learning process, preparation of feedback, evaluation of acquired knowledge and evaluation of the learning process.

Serious games design is implemented as a project in a course with a total of 8 ECTS credit points. In accordance with the provisions of the European Credit Transfer System students are supposed to spend between 220 to 240 h in the project activities. Course syllabus states that its main leaning goal is to summarize all didactic and technical knowledge that students acquired during their studies at the faculty and to apply it in a relatively complex project on instructional design. The course is based on the constructivist learning theory and has consequently very limited number of traditional lectures. In the introductory phase of the project lecturer presents main project requirements and defines some general rules about the learning goals and about organization of work in a project. Students get familiar with 'SADDIE' methodology that defines main project phases and other incidental activities.

Students work in groups of 3 or 4 students, which are set up according to their preferences. They are supposed to organize all activities in the project by themselves.

They are free to define different types of organizations of work and to accept different roles in the project. Later, during the run of the project, students in project groups write a log in which they report on the dynamics and organization of the work of the group. By analyzing the logs, we found that in some groups there were exposed leaders and in the others the responsibility was evenly distributed among all members.

At the regular weekly meetings groups prepare oral reports on the work in the past week and on any problems they have encountered. They receive immediate feedback from peers and from the teacher. If difficulties arise, the teacher initiates discussion about what could be the reasons for a problem and gives some hints or suggests possible ways to solve them.

3.2 Main Project Phases in SADDIE

As we have already mentioned, SADDIE methodology for serious games design and development consists of six main phases [15].

Specification. Specification is the initial phase of game design process. Students are supposed to choose the topic from the computer science syllabus for primary or secondary school, which is complex and challenging for the students, and consequently difficult to understand. Students have some experiences about such topics as they had four weeks of teaching practice in schools in the previous semesters. They have to consider if students could benefit from presenting the topic in a game format as game based learning is more time consuming that traditional learning and can only be justified when learning goals can not be reached otherwise. Students have to set didactic foundations for later stages of the project at this point and to define roughly some basics game elements such as time and place of the events, characters, artefacts, challenges, rules, and goals. Game should be funny and should provide competition or conflict.

After the initial phase students have to submit a document that contains a short presentation of the selected topic from syllabus with the arguments for the selection, a brief description of a gameplay, a list of specific learning goals from the official curriculum, motivational elements, specific game mechanics and didactical methods for achieving learning objectives, the methods for assessment of learning, tools for communication and collaborative work, and the suggestions for implementation of game into learning process.

Some examples of the selected topics in the previous years are binary numbers, arrays in programming language, the importance of sub-programs in programming, complexity of selected sorting algorithms, structural components of personal computers, rules of netiquette in the Internet, and Internet security threats.

Analysis. The analysis phase focuses on analysing the specification and preparing all the information needed for implementation phase. First decision is to select the target audience for the game that directs the choice of game story, level of difficulty, graphics, characters, interface, type of interactions and gameplay itself. Students have to consider available resources for implementing their ideas and make compromises. This includes selecting appropriate game engine, software for creating visual and audio artefacts and animations. Students have to focus on defining expected taxonomic levels of knowledge for selected learning goals. This is followed by the most important stage of analysis phase where learning goals are mapped onto game goals. It is crucial to include learning content in the game so that important elements are not lost and that the activities in the game do not override learning objectives. Objectives of the game should support an understanding of the main concepts in a different, more interesting way, which is familiar to the players and as such can facilitate the construction or transfer of knowledge. Progression throughout the game is possible only if player properly understand the concept behind game goal.

Design. The goals of a game can be associated with different types of knowledge. We are using the Kapp's taxonomy [7] that defines the following categories: declarative, conceptual, and procedural knowledge, knowledge based on rules and some other, so called 'soft skills'. Each goal of a game is evaluated based on this classification and incorporated into the story. Detailed scenarios are prepared in the design phase, with dialogues that integrate the requirements and recommendations from the specification phase. Students are then required to design all the graphical elements needed for the games, such as the backgrounds for the scenes, the artefacts, and all characters. They are also encouraged to record speech, sounds, and music for the game and to make simple animations.

Development. In the development phase, a game is produced with the selected game engine. When we started with educational game projects five years ago, students had to implement their own game engines with Actionscript 3 and produce the final product. We noticed that they spent a lot of time and energy on programming, so they couldn't focus so much on the content and didactical challenges. Our idea was to find the most appropriate game engine that would ease and fasten the development process. We decided to choose the e-Adventure platform, which has been developed in a research project aiming to facilitate the production of educational games at the Universidad Compultense de Madrid. It provides efficient tools for developing complex adventure games with just basic understanding of programming.

Implementation. Implementation phase defines various possibilities on how to incorporate learning with educational game into a learning process. Students have to consider different options and write specific proposals for teachers. It is crucial to find reasonable situations where learning outcomes can hardly be achieved using traditional teaching methods. Usually different accompanying activities need to be prepared as a learning package. Students carry out all these activities during their practical training in schools.

Evaluation and Testing. The evaluation phase is taking place in parallel with the implementation or immediately after this phase. Each project group prepares beta testing that is carried out by their peers. This is followed by gamma testing during their practice in primary or secondary schools. Students measure the efficiency of the alternative learning approach, comparing it to the traditional one, and they get feedback from the players and from teachers. This allows them to find out whether the objectives from specifications have been achieved and to improve the quality of their products.

3.3 Achieving Teaching Competences

SADDIE method is designed to stimulate improvement of different teaching competences in the courses in teacher education study programs through instructional design process [15]. Students achieve *didactic competences, technical competences,* and essential *skills for teamwork*. Didactic competences consist of reflective consideration on selection of learning goals, classification of learning goals according to taxonomic levels and type of knowledge, selection of appropriate activities for knowledge construction on selected taxonomic level, identification of suitable concept behind learning objective, ability to map the core idea into another context, and provision of proper feedback. Students also get familiar with the methodologies for evaluation of their work, acquired knowledge, and learning process.

Another key issue is the integration of serious game into teaching and learning process. Method of incorporation of games into the learning process depends on several factors and is specific to each game. The general problem is that the time available for a gameplay is limited. Therefore, it makes sense to use games only in the cases where it is difficult to achieve learning objectives with traditional methods. Students often then play serious games at home. It is very important that after such "homework" teachers plan appropriate reflection activities in the classroom. Without such activities in game-based learning does not lead to the expected results.

The activities in the framework of SADDIE process are not focused on technical aspects of a game design, but students usually become motivated during their project activities and they individually, with some support from teaching assistants, learn about animation, manipulation of visual materials, recording and editing music and other sounds, drawing in perspective, and learning more advanced programming techniques in order to make their projects more interesting.

The ability to work in a team is a relevant competence nowadays. It is very important for teachers to have this competency and that is why we pay special attention to it. Groups report on their collaboration experience in weekly meetings and all important activities and reflexions are collected in the log, which is written by each group during the project.

4 Conclusions

Active learning approach based on serious game design has been developed at the Faculty of Education, University of Ljubljana. Teacher students in the fourth year of the undergraduate study program *Two subjects teacher* design in develop educational games in small groups in projects that are carried out in the framework of the two-semester course *Application of ICT in education*. The methodology for this approach has been developed and its application in the last six years had various positive outcomes. Serious games as final products are just a side effect of the more important goal, i.e. achieving different competences that are essential for modern teachers. Vital teachers' competences include the ability to define learning goals that are in line with the syllabus, the choice of suitable didactical methods and their inclusion in the teaching process, development of a game, preparation of response for students, evaluation of acquired knowledge and of the learning process, independent planning and organization of all necessary activities in a project, and the ability for teamwork.

We have spread the use of this method to several elective courses at our university, to a course at the University of Rijeka, Croatia, and to postgraduate international summer schools on game based learning all around Europe.

References

1. Baptista R., Vaz de Carvalho, C.: Role play gaming and learning. Learn. Technol. **12**(1), 26–28 (2010)
2. Forest, E.: The ADDIE Model: Instructional Design. Frameworks and Theories. http://educationaltechnology.net/the-addie-model-instructional-design
3. Garris, R., Ahlers, R., Driskell, J.E.: Games, motivation, and learning: A research and practice model. Sim. Gaming **33**(4), 441–467 (2002)
4. Gee, J.P.: What Video Games Have to Teach Us About Learning and Literacy. Palgrave/Macmillan, New York (2003)
5. Gee, J.P.: Are video games good for learning? Curriculum Leader. J., **5**(1) (2007)
6. Gross, B.: The impact of videogames in education. First Monday **8**(7) (2003)
7. Kapp, K.M.: The Gamification of Learning and Instruction: Game-based Methods and Strategies for Training and Education. Pfeiffer, San Francisco (2012)
8. Malone, T.W.: Toward a theory of intrinsically motivating instruction. Cogn. Sci. **4**, 333–369 (1981)
9. Ormrod, J.E.: How Motivation Affects Learning and Behavior. Pearson Allyn & Bacon Prentice Hall, Boston (2010)
10. Pivec, M., Kearney, P.: Games for learning and learning from games. Informatica **31**, 419–423 (2007)
11. Prensky, M.: Digital natives, digital immigrants - Part 1. On the Horizon **9**(5), 1–6 (2001)
12. Prensky, M.: Digital Game-based Learning. McGraw-Hill, New York (2001)
13. Redecker, C., Ala-Mutka, K., Bacigalupo, M., Ferrari, A., Punie, Y.: Learning 2.0: The impact of Web 2.0 innovations on education and training in Europe. European Commission-Joint Research Center-Institute for Perspective Technological Studies, Seville (2009)
14. Rieber, L.P., Smith, L., Noah, D.: The value of serious play. Educ. Technol. **38**(6), 29–37 (1998)
15. Rugelj, J., Zapušek, M.: Achieving teacher's competencies in the serious games design process. In: Busch, C. (Ed.) Proceedings of the 8th European Conference on Games Based Learning ECGBL 2014. Academic Conferences and Publishing International Limited, Sonning Common (2014)
16. Shute, V.: Focus on formative feedback. Rev. Educ. Res. **78**(1), 154–189 (2008)
17. Shute, V.J., Ke, F.: Games, learning, and assessment. In: Ifenthaler, D., Eseryel, D., Ge, X. (eds.) Assessment in Game-Based Learning: Foundations, Innovations, and Perspective. Springer, New York (2012)
18. Shute, V.J., Rieber, L.P., Van Ec, K.R.: Games … and … learning. In: Dempsey, R.A. (ed.) Trends and Issues in Instructional Design and Technology, 3rd edn, pp. 321–332. Pearson Education, Boston (2012)
19. Van Eck, R.: Digital game-based learning: it's not just the digital natives who are restless. EDUCAUSE Rev. **41**(2), 16 (2006)

20. Whitton, N.: Learning with Digital Games: A Practical Guide to Engaging Students in Higher Education. Routledge, New York (2009)
21. Zapušek, M., Cerar, Š., Rugelj, J.: Serious computer games as instructional technology. In: Čičin-Šain, M. (ed.) Proceedings of MIPRO 2011 Computers in Education, vol. 4, pp. 93–95. MIPRO, Rijeka (2011)
22. Zapušek, M., Rugelj, J.: Learning programming with serious games. EAI Endorsed Trans. Game Based Learn. **13**(01), e6 (2013)

Enabling Control of 3D Visuals, Scenarios and Non-linear Gameplay in Serious Game Development Through Model-Driven Authoring

Sofie Van Hoecke[1](✉), Koen Samyn[2], Gaétan Deglorie[1], Olivier Janssens[1], Peter Lambert[1], and Rik Van de Walle[1]

[1] Multimedia Lab, ELIS, Ghent University-iMinds, Ghent, Belgium
sofie.vanhoecke@ugent.be

[2] DAE, University College of West-Flanders, Kortrijk, Belgium
koen.samyn@howest.be

Abstract. Due to the absence of high-level authoring environments and support for non-technical domain experts to create custom serious games, a model-driven authoring framework is presented in this paper. Through model-driven authoring, non-technical people can manipulate the 3D visuals of their serious game, model the scenarios of the game, and even easily add non-linear narrative to the game. The different tools and methods have been implemented and are currently used to build a serious game for the Friendly ATTAC project in order to help youngsters who are confronted with cyberbullying. The presented model-driven authoring framework enables non-technical domain experts to produce serious games easily and quickly, at a lower cost, and therefore lowers the barriers that hinder the production of serious games.

Keywords: Serious game · Cyberbullying · Adaptivity · Scenario generation · Non-linear gameplay · Sandbox · Model-driven authoring

1 Introduction

Serious games are games considered to be both educational and fun. The need is raised for high-level authoring environments in order to (1) allow people without professional game design skills to create or modify serious games [1], and (2) enhance serious game development as development costs are one of the major drawbacks [2].

To solve this shortcoming, this paper presents a model-driven authoring framework that enables non-technical domain experts to produce serious games easily and quickly, at lower cost, and therefore lowers the barriers that hinder the production of serious games. The authoring framework is used within the Friendly ATTAC project, in which an innovative serious game is developed to help youngsters deal with cyberbullying (bullying via electronic communication tools) by focussing on the bystander behavior. Cyberbullying is a relatively recent phenomenon that especially occurs among early adolescents (12–15 year olds).

C. Vaz de Carvalho et al. (Eds.): SGAMES 2015, LNICST 161, pp. 103–110, 2016.
DOI: 10.1007/978-3-319-29060-7_16

As it may have a serious impact on the mental (and physical) wellbeing of victims, many societal actors are currently involved in anti-cyberbullying initiatives. They strongly plea for evidence-based, appealing serious games that empower youngsters confronted with cyberbullying.

The remainder of this paper is as follows. Section 2 outlines the general concept of our model-driven authoring framework that semi-automatically translates theoretical and empirical knowledge into attractive virtual scenarios and allows to add non-linear narrative. The subsections describe the steps of the process in more detail. After presenting screenshots and video footage of the resulting game against cyberbullying in Sects. 3, 4 summarizes our work.

2 Model-Driven Authoring Framework

Figure 1 presents the general concept of our model-driven authoring framework. Several steps have to be followed in order to generate scenarios and levels for the serious game. Firstly, social scientists have to write scenarios which incorporate their theories and hypotheses they want to test or model. Secondly, via the authoring framework they can translate their scenarios into ATTAC-L scenarios and add non-linear narrative. The ATTAC-L language is a graphically illustrated modelling language for educational virtual scenarios, understandable by non-technical people. In parallel, they can model the visual aspects of the game levels using our own sandbox that offers features tailored to the development of serious games. The third step consists of the XML file generation based on the ATTAC-L scenarios on one hand and the sandbox configuration on the other hand. The fourth step takes the XML file and translates it into actual game level and moves.

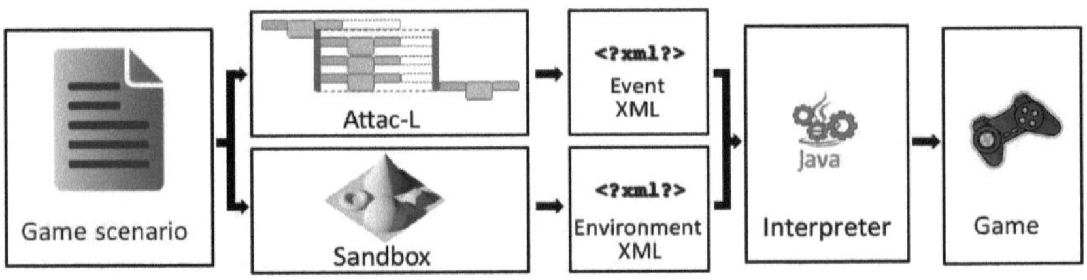

Fig. 1. General concept of process to generate game scenarios and levels

In the next subsections, the different steps of the process are described in more detail. First, we define how scenarios and game levels can be designed using ATTAC-L. Second, we describe how non-linear narrative can be generated in order to adapt the gameplay at runtime based on the player's progress. Third, we describe the sandbox to manipulate the 3D elements of the game. Finally, the produced XML files of these three steps are translated by the interpreter into actual game levels and moves.

2.1 Designing the Scenarios and Levels Using ATTAC-L

A domain-specific modeling language, called ATTAC-L, is developed within the Friendly ATTAC project [6] to accommodate domain experts in the design process of scenarios and allow the semi-automatically creation of serious games.

By using the ATTAC-L control structures such as communication, sequence, choice and concurrency structures, it is possible to create entire scenarios and game levels in ATTAC-L. For more information on the scenario generation using this ATTAC-L, the reader is referred to [7]. Once the scenarios and levels are constructed in ATTAC-L, they are translated to an XML file in the back-end of the authoring framework.

2.2 Adding Non-linear Narrative with Scenario Templates

Non-linear gameplay is needed to provide an optimal learning experience and teach certain behaviour or knowledge to the users of the serious game by adapting the gameplay based on the real-time player input or post-game feedback. Therefore, a story engine is created that selects a scenario template from a scenario database based on the current state of the player model and provides the template with contextual information from the game. The story engine is also responsible for maintaining the integrity of the storyline, defined by additional metadata in the templates. This way, the player's learning state can be tracked in real-time and used to adapt the gameplay and occurence of learning challenges in order to better suit the problem areas of the player. An overview of the story engine is presented in Fig. 2.

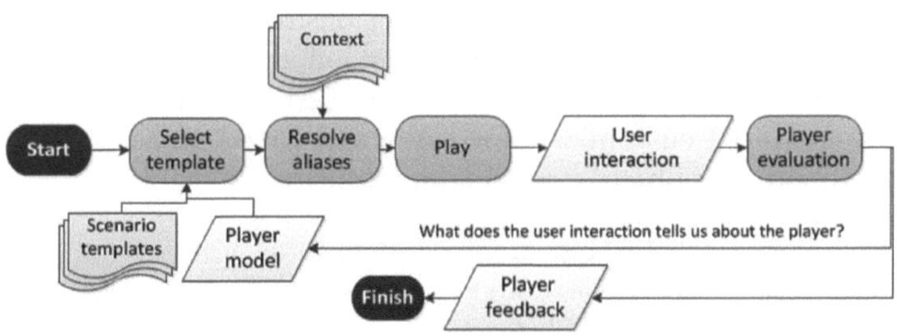

Fig. 2. Story engine overview

When the game requires the start of a new scenario, a scenario is selected from a database of scenario templates. The selection process takes the current state of the player model (i.e. the relative skill of the player in each of the specific learning challenges) into account, including the previous actions and the current location of the player. The scenario might also require the proximity or availability of non-player characters (NPC's). Furthermore the scenario might define the characteristics (traits and facets) of these NPC's. Once a scenario is selected, the aliases in the template are replaced with the appropriate and currently available NPC's and/or items. The scenario template can require an NPC, with a predefined set of personality characteristics (e.g. bully trait vs victim of bullying), and/or a specific state from the player model. Next the actions in the scenario are played or executed, and possible options are presented to the player. The decision of the player will trigger an evaluation and leads to an update of the player model. The player model is used to adapt the probability that a given scenario template will be selected, given the performance objective to which it belongs. For more information on generating non-linear narrative of serious games using these scenario templates, the reader is referred to [8].

2.3 Sandbox

Most game engines provide developers with a sandbox, i.e. an environment in which the 3D elements of a game can be manipulated. The sandbox is typically tightly coupled with the features of the game engine and this introduces two major problems for serious game development. The first problem is that extending the game engine to make it suitable for serious game development is not trivial. Another problem is that efforts are mostly non portable. As a result, a game developed within sandbox A for game engine A cannot easily be converted to run on another game engine.

Within our model-driven authoring framework, we also want to describe the visual aspects of the game in a model driven manner in order to solve the two mentioned problems. We therefore introduce our own sandbox that offers features tailored to the development of serious games. The sandbox exports the serious game levels as XML files, but it also possible to extend the sandbox by writing a plug-in that exports the sandbox in another desired file format.

The properties and actions that an object offers are described in an XML file. An example of such a descriptor is given in Listing 1. This descriptor makes it possible to create UI customizers for every supported object, but also to add new features to existing objects, or to add an entirely new object.

Listing 1. Object descriptor

```
<object label="Sound" class="dae.prefabs.standard.SoundEntity">
    <parameters section="Transform">
        <parameter type="string"  id="name"/>
        <parameter type="float3"  id="localTranslation"/>
        <parameter type="sound"   id="soundFile"/>
        <parameter type="range"   id="volume" min="0" max="10" step="0.1"/>
        <parameter type="boolean" id="looping"/>
        <parameter type="boolean" id="positional"/>
        <parameter type="action"  id="playSound" method="playSound"/>
    </parameters>
</object>
```

Aside from the basic features that every sandbox must possess, our solution focuses on users with limited or no skill with regards to the creation of a 3D virtual world. Therefore care has been taken to provide the users with sufficient tools to place and manipulate objects. An example of such a tool is the *insert object tool* which uses ray casting to make it easier to quickly "drop" an object on the scene. The tool can also take the surface of the current scene into account to create a perfect alignment (e.g. placing an object on a ramp). Another example is the lighting tool which shows the changes to lighting in real time. A demonstration of these features and more can be seen on http://youtu.be/F37eCIz8Xyg.

An additional feature of the sandbox is the layer and level system, allowing users to quickly switch from one context to another. Items like lights, way points, trigger boxes and paths are automatically put in separate layers. Switching a layer's visibility on and off makes it easier to manage an entire level.

Finally, the sandbox design is extensible. The object system makes it possible to define new components that can be attached to existing objects. For example, for the Friendly ATTAC project, it is necessary to add trait and personality information to NPC's. Listing 2 shows the method to define the UI customizers for such a 'Personality' component. A demonstration of adding this 'Personality' component, a path, physics and animation to characters is presented in http://youtu.be/u7jBSJ7c4nY.

Listing 2. Define component

```
<component id="Personality" class="dae.characters.Personality">
    <!-- add customizers for personality component -->
    <parameters section="Personality">
        <parameter type="range" id="bully" min="0" max="10" step="0.1"/>
        <parameter type="range" id="friendly" min="0" max="10" step="0.1"/>
    </parameters>
</component>
```

The addition or removal of components from an object will affect all the existing objects of the same type. This way, useful components can be reused without the need to redefine the parameters.

Listing 3. Add component

```
<object id="NPC" class="dae.NPC">
    <components>
        <!-- add Personality component to every NPC object -->
        <component id="Personality" key="personality"/>
    </components>
    <parameters section="Transform">
        <parameter type="string" id="name"/>
        <parameter type="string" id="animation"/>
        <parameter type="string" id="actorName"/>
        <parameter type="string" id="actorId"/>
        <parameter type="float3" id="translation"/>
        <parameter type="float3" id="rotation"
            converter="QuaternionConverter"/>
    </parameters>
</object>
```

The resulting visuals aspects of the game levels are exported by the sandbox as XML files, and given to the code generator.

2.4 Interpreter

The constructed XML files of, on one hand, the scenarios, levels and scenario templates, and, on the other hand, the visual aspects of the game levels, are then used by our interpreter to translate them into actual game levels and moves using the in-engine format. This interpreter consists of hard-coded bridges between the ATTAC-L XML and the in-engine format of the game engine, and ensures that the correct scenarios and game moves are activated or executed based on the input and actions of the player. This way, the interpreter allows to hide the implementation details of the virtual world from the scenario writers.

3 Resulting Game Against Cyberbullying

As the Friendly ATTAC serious game focuses on helping youngsters deal with cyberbullying, a school context was chosen. This way, on one hand, the likelihood of impacting the social behavior of even poorly motivated youngsters increases, and, on the other hand, a nice game can be developed to draw their attention. The school context and characters of the Friendly ATTAC game are presented in Fig. 3. The resulting game is an online, single player, adaptive and personalised role-playing (RPG) detective game, called 'The Messenger'. The scenarios and interactions within the game are based on theoretical and empirical knowledge regarding personal and contextual determinants of cyberbullying, obtained by performing a well-established intervention method from the field of health psychology, i.e. Intervention Mapping (IM) [3]. The game attempts to modify behavior patterns of bullies, bystanders and victims by allowing youngsters, through the use of virtual scenarios, experience different roles (bully, victim, or bystander) in cyber bullying incidents, and to react to those experiences in order to get adjusted feedback based on their individual reactions. This way, we hope to make youngsters more aware of the consequences of certain behaviour (as a bully or as bystander) and help them to prevent becoming a victim. Bullies will be encouraged to cease bullying by increasing their empathy, victims will be taught adequate coping strategies and bystanders could be sensibilized to intervene. The model-driven authoring framework has been implemented and is currently used to build the different levels of the Friendly ATTAC game. Figure 4 shows some screenshots of the resulting game. Video footage can be seen at http://youtu.be/qwmLJzMdFzw.

Fig. 3. School context and characters of the Friendly ATTAC serious game

(a) Personalizing your character

(b) Player and storyboard device

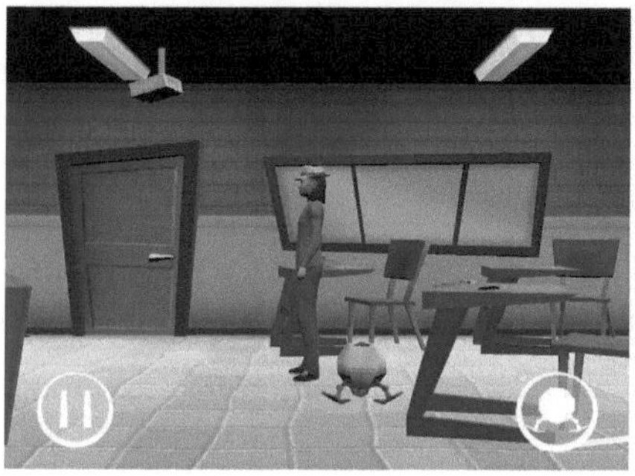

(c) Class room

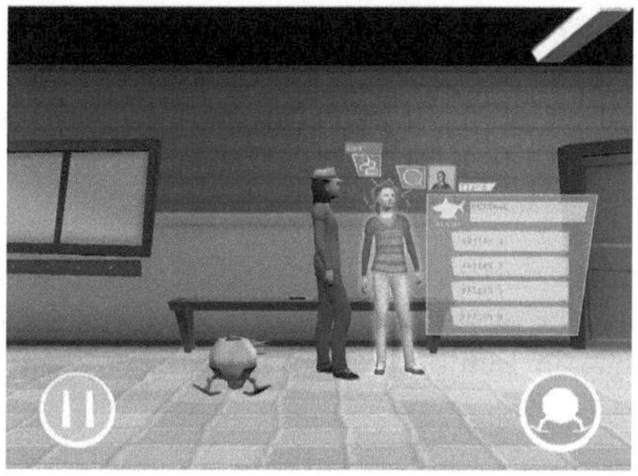

(d) Social interaction with NPC

Fig. 4. Screenshots of Friendly ATTAC serious game

4 Conclusions and Future Work

We presented a model-driven authoring framework that allows non-technical people to manipulate the 3D visuals, model the scenarios, and easily add non-linear narrative to the game. The different tools and methods have been implemented and are used to build a serious game for the Friendly ATTAC project in order to help youngsters confronted with cyberbullying.

By using a virtual game scenario generation process, it is possible for non-technical people to model virtual scenarios. Technical details are provided on how the scenarios can be modelled in ATTAC-L and afterwards be translated in computer interpretable XML. This XML is then used to automatically build the scenario and game moves within the game engine so that it can be played.

Non-linear narrative is introduced using scenario templates and aliasing. The aliasing approach facilitates the design process by using scenario templates as a way to create a dynamic experience with an individualized storyline inside the game. Specific to the topic of serious games and learning is the creation of a player-driven narrative that tests the player on his/her skills. This is achieved through the mapping of performance objectives to each scenario template using metadata and by creating a model of a player that is adapted towards.

Finally, by using the presented sandbox, the visual aspects of the game can be manipulated and described using XML, making our sandbox better tailored to the development of serious games.

The presented model-driven authoring framework enables non-technical domain experts to produce serious games easily and quickly, at a lower cost, and therefore lowers the barriers that hinder the production of serious games.

As for future work, improvements in several areas are envisioned. First, the vocabulary of ATTAC-L verbs will be expanded, allowing more actions to become possible in the game. Second, linked templates with smart selection will be implemented by populating the pool of available event templates only by those events that can follow the previous one. Third, our work focuses on the aliasing aspects of characters. However, a story may also require geographic bifurcations. E.g. the main character could choose a different path to reach the destination. In this case a scenario would not only contain aliases for characters but also for geographic locations (e.g. hidden caves, treasures, or bridges).

Acknowledgment. This work was funded by the IWT SBO Friendly ATTAC project, a project of the Institute for the Promotion of Innovation through Science and Technology in Flanders (IWT): http://www.friendlyattac.be

References

1. Djaouti, D., Alvarez, J., Jessel, J.P.: Can gaming 2.0 help design serious games? a comparative study. In: SIGGRAPH, Los Angeles, CA, USA (2010)
2. Bellotti, F., Berta, R., De Gloria, A.: Designing effective serious games: opportunities and challenges for research. Int. J. Emerg. Technol. Learn. **5**, 22–35 (2010)
3. Bartholomew, L.K., Parcel, G.S., Kok, G., Gottlieb, N.H., Fernandez, M.E.: Planning Health Promotion Programs: An Intervention Mapping Approach. Wiley, San Francisco (2011)
4. Aylett, R.S., Louchart, S., Dias, J., Paiva, A.C.R., Vala, M.: FearNot! - an experiment in emergent narrative. In: Panayiotopoulos, T., Gratch, J., Aylett, R.S., Ballin, D., Olivier, P., Rist, T. (eds.) IVA 2005. LNCS (LNAI), vol. 3661, pp. 305–316. Springer, Heidelberg (2005)
5. Riedl, M.O., Stern, A., Dini, D., Alderman, J.: Dynamic experience management in virtual worlds for entertainment, education, and training. Int. Trans. Syst. Sci. Appl., Special Issue on Agent Based Systems for Human Learning **4**(2), 23–42 (2008)
6. Van Broeckhoven, F., De Troyer, O.: ATTAC-L: a modeling language for educational virtual scenarios in the context of preventing cyber bullying. In: IEEE 2nd International Conference on Serious Games and Applications for Health (2013)
7. Janssens, O., Samyn, K., Van de Walle, R., Van Hoecke, S.: Educational virtual game scenario generation for serious games. In: IEEE 3rd International Conference on Serious Games and Applications for Health (2014)
8. Samyn, K., Deglorie, G., Lambert, P., Van de Walle, R., Van Hoecke, S.: Generating non-linear narrative for serious games with scenario templates. In: Proceedings of GRAPP, Berlin, Germany (2015)

Serious Games for Large-Scale Image Sensing

Bruno Simões[1(✉)], Michele Bianchi[2], Alberto Debiasi[1], and Raffaele De Amicis[1]

[1] Graphitech, Trento, Italy
{bruno.simoes,alberto.debiasi,raffaele.de.amicis}@graphitech.it
[2] University of Trento, Trento, Italy

Abstract. The access to large-scale imagery datasets has been a significant obstacle to the success of many applications in application domains that range from 3D modelling to augmented reality, and from infrastructure inspection to urban planning. Although large collections of images already exist, from sources such as Bing Maps, Google Street View, and many photo-sharing sites, they are incomplete, inaccurate and expensive. A solution to this problem could be to leverage on large end-user communities to collaboratively acquire and share information about their surroundings. In this paper, we outline some basic mechanics in serious games that can be explored for the purpose of data collection. Additionally, we describe new ways of guiding players' actions towards the purpose of our game – image and video crowdsourcing.

Keywords: Serious games methodologies · Participatory sensing

1 Introduction

The ubiquity of full-fledged sensing, computing, and communication devices like smartphones is paving the wave for new perspectives on how to accomplish large-scale sensing. The phenomenon of large-scale sensing, which is better known in the literature as participatory sensing, is an approach to data collection and analysis in which individuals and communities use their personal devices to acquire and explore specific aspects of their surroundings. The number of applications is quite vast and can range from environmental issues to culture. Imagine, for example, that we are capable of collecting geo-referred images and videos that depict every single corner of a town, at different times of the day and year. Then we could use our framework [1] to reconstruct any object (e.g. animals, buildings, etc.) and even entire cities in 4D (a 3D model with a time dimension), with the use of computer vision techniques. The potential of these 4D representations is huge. We could create virtual tours that would enable users to visit or explore new parts of a town without going there; in addition to experience it from any location and angle, at any specific time of the day or the year (e.g. day, night, winter, summer, etc.). It would enable us to preserve and experience moments like when a building is torn down, repaired or constructed, outdoor festivals, etc. This data could also be ingested by domain-specific applications in order to

C. Vaz de Carvalho et al. (Eds.): SGAMES 2015, LNICST 161, pp. 111–118, 2016.
DOI: 10.1007/978-3-319-29060-7_17

support their users monitoring and analysing, for example, the infrastructure of a building, for urban planning, or simply for the benefit of individual creators or creative industries (e.g. operating in 3D game content creation).

There are a couple of online services that provide access to large structured (e.g., Bing Maps, Google Street View, etc) and unstructured collections of images (Flickr, Picasa, Panoramio, Facebook). However, these repositories have several drawbacks if used in the aforementioned context. One the one hand, acquiring imagery from structured repositories can be financially expensive – structured repositories are often the core business of commercial enterprises. Additionally, data is only available in certain areas or it captures only certain features of the environment, e.g. streets. Another issue is that these repositories are updated very sporadically, thus, these collections may be out of date at some point; similarly, these collections maintain only a specific moment of day or of the year – e.g. when the last satellite picture was taken. On the other hand, we can find many unstructured repositories that are maintained by thousands of people that walk around everyday with devices that can take pictures or record videos. The only flaw in these services is that only the most attractive facades of landmarks are well-represented, against everything else that is very sparsely captured.

In our applicational context, this limitation represents a serious issue because to create 4D models of complex scenes or objects (e.g. a concert or the building appearance spanning across many years) we need to find an sustainable approach that enable us to collect the vast number of 'missing' view angles, along the time span we want to reconstruct, and without any special equipment. So far, many crowdsourcing applications have been developed. However, crowdsourcing applications have first to overcome the challenge of how to motivate massive crowds to participate. There are two main strategies that are widely used to influence user behaviour towards doing a specific action: serious games and gamification. Serious games are "games that do not have entertainment, enjoyment or fun as their primary purpose" [2,3]. Gamification is primarily characterised by the fact that the game, if defined, is always secondary to the tasks that have to be performed, e.g. adding a points system, peer pressure, leaderboards, as well as other things that normally would not be considered. Effective gamification exploits the user context to provide motivation specific to the situation, instead of simple integration of badges and leaderboards [4,5].

In this paper, we introduce a serious game to crowdsource the gathering of videos and pictures. Our key contribution is the game design that is proposed. In our game, the simple action of taking pictures serves two purposes: players perceive it as a mechanism to capture magical creatures; from our perspective it is a strategy to gather pictures. The outcome of the game, which is transparent to the gameplay, is a set of images spanning over large areas, from multiple angles, and a set of 4D models reconstructed from those images.

2 Related Work

The idea behind Serious Games (SG) is to design them so they provide entertainment to the players while primarily serving a greater purpose. The purpose of the game can be to generate useful data, to communicate information, to teach concept. Most serious games are based on the work of von Ahn, who developed together with other authors the ESP game [6] and Peekaboom [7] to demonstrate the concept, along with other widely used games [8,9]. The ESP game was designed for the purpose of labelling random Internet pictures. The game is grounded on the idea that whenever two players visualise the same image they should come up with textual tags that match. In this game, players are paired randomly without any means of communication; therefore to earn points, they must find tags that most people would associate to the image. Peekaboom, on the other hand, involves defining the location of objects.

Foldit [10] is an experiment that serves to exemplify the relevance and efficiency of using games that take advantage of human' innate spatial reasoning abilities, to solve problems that computers fail to resolve. In this game, people can help research scientists to solve a protein-folding problem that had baffled them for more than a decade. The objective of the game is to find, for each digital 3D protein structure, the most tightly packed configuration.

Astro Drone [11] is another crowdsourcing effort based on data collection through a game. The aim of the game is to play a spaceship simulation game in which players have to control a spacecraft that has to fly close to a comet and then release a lander on it. The game sends the data extracted from the camera of the drone to ESA to be then used in the study of new automatic control systems (e.g. obstacles avoidance and docking).

PhotoCity [12] is a game with the purpose of collecting photos. This game relies on small groups of expert photographers highly motivated to acquire pictures that are useful to the reconstruction of buildings. Players are rewarded with castles and flags as they contribute to 3D replicas. The authors used vision techniques to reward only those players with useful input. The drawback of this strategy is that this game is designed to reward only those players with exceptional skills in photography, as a way to compensate for a limitation in their 3D reconstruction framework. Consequently, the game fails to implement a mechanism that can attract large communities and that can maintain them engaged independently of their skills or interests.

Finally, EyeSpy is another relevant game that proposed by Bell et al. [13]. The objective of this game is to collect pictures and tags that can be functional in a navigational context, for example, to give directions to someone based on landmarks that can be easily recognisable. To play the game, we just need to walk around, take pictures, and insert tags. Additionally, the player can geolocate and tag pictures collected by other players.

3 Methodology

Our game is split into three game moments: capturing creatures, exchanging cards and fighting other players. Capturing creatures requires players to go outdoors and use their smartphones in AR mode, see Sect. 3.4. There are two strategies for capturing creatures: take a picture to a spot that was identified directly through the display or by "blindly" taking pictures around – to discover hidden gems. The game provides also a tool to assess the "elemental profile" of a physical location, which determines the probabilities of capturing a creature of a specific element and a radar for navigational purposes.

In this game, creatures are quite abundant in quantity but not in quality. As we will explain later, during game battles weak creatures will be absorbed by other creatures either to attack or to evolve. This mechanic was integrated to push players into taking pictures even if they do not need more creatures. It also generates dynamics that appeal to explorers user-type whom are looking to complete their list of creatures, and to killer user-type that want to gain the upper hand against others, e.g. influence points.

Fighting pits two players one against another for the supremacy of a guild over another, that is, for influence points. Players will have to use creatures they have captured in order to win. There are two different ways of engaging in a battle: (1) the player requests a online fight or (2) the game automatically initiates a fight between two players. The latter, called proximity battle, forces players to fight each other if they are capturing creatures in the same zone. Players can withdraw by paying a certain number of elemental cards or alternatively by sacrificing a creature.

A creature can be summon only after the DNA (picture) of the creature is uploaded to our backend infrastructure – an action that corresponds to reconstruct the creature from its DNA. We implemented this strategy of unlocking creatures at home or via WIFI to avoid exceeding their data plans. At the backend, we assess the veracity as well as the added value provided by the picture, which is a parameter in the computation of the set of abilities that is assigned to the creature.

In the next sections, we describe the most crucial gameplay elements in conjunction with the effect they should generate on the collection of pictures during the intervention.

3.1 Creatures' Distribution and Elemental Affinity

Creatures are aligned to one or more fictional elements that have been selected for the game. Each player character (selected during the registration process) has a stronger affinity to a pair of elements and a weaker affinity to a third element. Affinities change the probability of finding creatures of those elements, making it easier for elements with a stronger affinity and harder for elements with a weaker affinity. Nevertheless, this property does not change the fact that some elements are incompatible with certain environments. For example, fire-based creatures are unlikely to be spotted inside lakes, see Sect. 3.2 for more details.

To further push the interaction between players and to balance the way players can earn influence points, cities (physical space) and towns are automatically sub-divided into zones. The size of each zone in the spatial grid is inversely proportional to the number of pictures taken in the surrounding area, following the concept of a quad-tree. The purpose of this mechanism is to balance the spatial distribution of pictures and consequently to control the way players can earn points. However, players shall perceive it differently: when a player captures a creature the control of that guild in that specific zone is increased (influence points). This new probability of finding a creature is presented as a decrease in the population of creatures (localised). The population is automatically restored over time, based on players behaviour or on external factors (e.g. an happening, a festival, etc.). Restoration over time has designed for continuous player involvement: newbies can always find a place to go for hunting, while veteran players are required to return regularly to their zones in order to maintain their local influence points. This strategy attracts not only the attention of killers and achievers player types [14,15], but also of achievers and explorers that are interested in finding rare gems where elements have not been depleted. The location and bearing of a picture within a zone are two of most relevant variables used to compute the probability of finding strong creatures, see Section. An internal algorithm was implemented to balance the scores by comparing these properties at local and global level – players always compete with someone.

3.2 Creatures' Habitat and Elemental Affinity

To maximise the realism of our game and to attract explorer-type players, we have implemented a service that constrains the probability of finding specific creatures in certain areas. Hence, marine creatures are most likely to be found nearby the sea and an elf nearby a forest. The game procedure is fully automatic, however, at the moment it supports only the European territory.

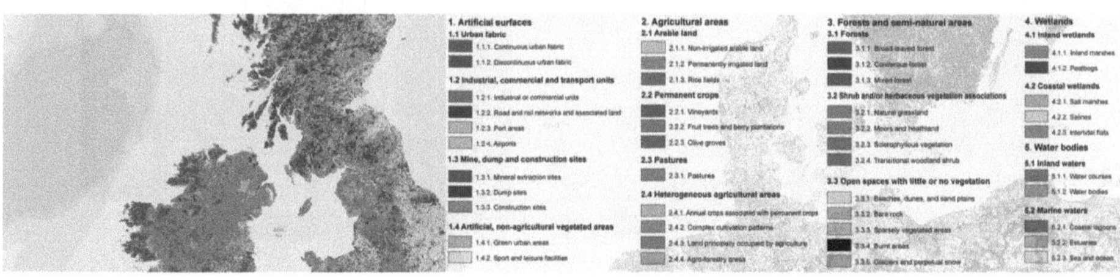

Fig. 1. Corine land cover.

The habitat mapping service is engineered as a two layers data service. The first data layer exposes the Corine Land Cover (CLC) of Europe as a service. The CLC nomenclature aggregates 44 land cover classes in a three-level hierarchy. Five main categories are "artificial surfaces", "agricultural areas", "forest and semi-natural areas", "wetlands" and "water bodies", see Fig. 1. The second data layer requests, to the first layer, the CLC code of a given location and then computes the list of compatible elements to that nomenclature.

The number of new creatures that is generated depends on the relevance of the area. Our system is capable of generating thousands of different creatures and descriptions without human intervention. During the creation process the system takes into account the strategies described above. Every time a new card is generated, we have to update the database of the living creatures. See Sect. 3.4 for a few examples of automatically generated cards. Limited and thematic editions will also be considered.

3.3 Creatures Lifecycle

Given that many of our mechanics are based on probabilistic algorithms, both for generating and combining creatures, we have implemented an ageing effect – creatures will age and die – to prevent the use of singularities in fights. Creatures will age one year (creature's calendar) for each week (player's calendar). After a certain number of years ($\exists n \in \mathbb{N}, 2^n = i$, where i is the age of the card in weeks) the creature goes through an elemental evolution. At each evolution, the player can decide which element of the creature to level-up. A creature can live up to 110 years in average. Players can capture creatures with ages raging from 10 to 40 years old. Under special conditions, e.g. legendary creatures that correspond to high-value pictures, creatures can live up to 390 years.

The maximum lifespan of a creature is also shortened after each battle by one year. However, as a recompense, creatures evolve whenever the condition $\gcd(n, F_{n+1}) > 2$ is satisfied. The sum of all battles is represented by n; F is the Fibonacci Sequence and gcd is the greatest common divisor.

Fig. 2. Left: augmented reality interface. Right: collectible creatures.

Figure 2 depicts the interface to find creatures and market places, where creatures can be exchanged. By taking a picture the user accesses the closest and most central icon on the display.

3.4 Combat Mechanics

The game battle between players is split into 4 game moments: (1) summoning, (2) energy infusion, (3) energy release, and finally, (4) defence release. At the beginning of each turn – step 1 – players can summon new creatures into the battlefield. Players are free to pick the creature they want from their deck. The cost of the second phase – energy infusion – depends on the number and type of cards that are on the battlefield: creatures in the battlefield will absorb cards from the player' deck until they collect the number (and type) of elements that are indicated in their properties. Creatures in the battlefield can also be sacrificed for this purpose. In a third phase – energy release – we take all creature' elements that are levelled-up as the player' magical attack. In step 4, the defender will have to infuse any missing elements (quality and quantity) from their deck to match the opponents attack. The first player to run out of cards looses the match as well as a percentage of the cards absorbed. The battlefield itself will have affinity to a few elements – that depends on the players' location or that is otherwise random – that changes the properties of an element to: double effect, no effect, or half effect.

Lastly, the game page features a leader board where players are ranked by influence points. There are five titles that players can earn: The Warlord (won the largest number of battles), The Expeditioner (possesses the largest number of gems), The Imperator (rules the largest number of areas), and The Evangelist (manage to convince the highest number of users to play the game). Local-level titles were also defined.

4 Conclusion

This paper describes the design of a serious game that aims at motivate players to take pictures, so they can be used for 3D reconstruction purposes. The game was designed to attract different types of players' personality. We archived this by integrating the use of different game play strategies, e.g. engaging in combats, collecting cards, exploring physical spaces, including social interactions, etc. The design of mechanisms to deal with sparse sensing and to evaluating data trustworthiness were among our biggest considerations.

In future work we have to compare the performance of our pure crowdsourcing application with this game-based strategy. We also have to investigate how to improve the security and reliability of the framework and how to handle intellectual property and privacy issues, e.g. reconstruction a person without the proper permission.

Acknowledgements. This research has been supported by the European Commission (EC) under the project c-Space (Grant Agreement N. 611040). The authors are solely responsible for the content of the paper. It does not represent the opinion of the European Community. The European Community is not responsible for any use that might be made of information contained herein. Special thanks should also be given to Matteo Eccher (Graphitech), Luca Baldesi (University of Trento), and Laura Cattoni (MUSE) for their contribution to the gameplay mentioned in this paper.

References

1. Simões, B., De Amicis, R.: Digital earth in a user-centric perspective. In: Fifth International Conference on Computing for Geospatial Research and Application (COM. Geo), pp. 47–48. IEEE (2014)

2. Michael, D.R., Chen. S.L.: Serious Games: Games That Educate, Train, and Inform. Muska & Lipman/Premier-Trade (2005)
3. Djaouti, D., Alvarez, J., Jessel, J.-P., Rampnoux, O.: Origins of serious games. In: Ma, M., Oikonomou, A., Jain, L.C. (eds.) Serious Games and Edutainment Applications, pp. 25–43. Springer, London (2011)
4. Marczewski, A.: Gamification: A Simple Introduction. Andrzej Marczewski (2012)
5. Zichermann, G., Linder, J.: The Gamification Revolution. Mcgraw-Hill Professional, Berkeley (2013)
6. Von Ahn, L., Dabbish, L.: Labeling images with a computer game. In: Proceedings of the SIGCHI Conference on Human Factors in Computing Systems, pp. 319–326. ACM (2004)
7. Von Ahn, L., Liu, R., Blum, M.: Peekaboom: a game for locating objects in images. In: Proceedings of the SIGCHI Conference on Human Factors in Computing Systems, pp. 55–64. ACM (2006)
8. Von Ahn, L., Ginosar, S., Kedia, M., Blum, M.: Improving image search with phetch. In: IEEE International Conference on Acoustics, Speech and Signal Processing, ICAAAP 2007, vol. 4, p. IV-1209. IEEE (2007)
9. Eickhoff, C., Harris, C.G., de Vries, A.P., Srinivasan, P.: Quality through flow, immersion: gamifying crowdsourced relevance assessments. In: Proceedings of the 35th International ACM SIGIR Conference on Research and Development in Information Retrieval, pp. 871–880. ACM (2012)
10. Cooper, S., Khatib, F., Treuille, A., Barbero, J., Lee, J., Beenen, M., Leaver-Fay, A., Baker, D., Popović, Z., et al.: Predicting protein structures with a multiplayer online game. Nature **466**(7307), 756–760 (2010)
11. de Croon, G., Gerke, P.K., Sprinkhuizen-Kuyper, I.: Crowdsourcing as a methodology to obtain large and varied robotic data sets. In: 2014 IEEE/RSJ International Conference on Intelligent Robots and Systems (IROS 2014), pp. 1595–1600. IEEE (2014)
12. Tuite, K., Snavely, N., Hsiao, D.-Y., Tabing, N., Popovic, Z.: Photocity: training experts at large-scale image acquisition through a competitive game. In: Proceedings of the SIGCHI Conference on Human Factors in Computing Systems, CHI 2011, pp. 1383–1392. ACM, New York (2011). http://doi.acm.org/10.1145/1978942.1979146
13. Bell, M., Reeves, S., Brown, B., Sherwood, S., MacMillan, D., Ferguson, J., Chalmers, M.: Eyespy: supporting navigation through play. In: Proceedings of the SIGCHI Conference on Human Factors in Computing Systems, pp. 123–132. ACM (2009)
14. Bartle, R.: Hearts, clubs, diamonds, spades: players who suit muds. J. MUD Res. **1**(1), 19 (1996)
15. Stewart, B.: Personality, play styles: a unified model. Gamasutra (2011). http://www.gamasutra.com/view/feature/6474/personality_and_play_styles_a_.php

Games' "Social Tech Booster"

Tiago Cardoso[1(✉)], Vitor Santos[2], Carolina Santos[3], and José Barata[1]

[1] CTS – Uninova, Departamento de Engenharia Electrotécnica, Faculdade de Ciências e Tecnologias, Universidade Nova de Lisboa, campus Monte da Caparica, Caparica, Portugal
{tomfc,jab}@uninova.pt

[2] Instituto Superior de Estatística e Gestão de Informação, Universidade Nova de Lisboa, Lisbon, Portugal
vsantos@isegi.unl.pt

[3] Escola Nacional de Saúde Pública, Universidade Nova de Lisboa, Lisbon, Portugal
c.santos@ensp.unl.pt

Abstract. The society has organized itself towards facing existing social needs like the care for children with Down syndrome, Deafness or Autism Spectrum Disorders, among several other pathologies. As a result, several organizations emerged towards handling these issues, composed of doctors, therapists, psychologists, among other professionals, but excluding technology experts. On the other hand side, the finalist students from technology universities usually have a final course where they have to create a complete project from scratch. This article proposes a method for applying the effort and enthusiasm of such students in the above mentioned social causes through games' development.

Keywords: Social games · Deafness · Autism Spectrum Disorders · Down syndrome

1 Introduction

Children that are born with "differences" have a large set of Social Care Structures (SCS) created by the society that help to take care of such "differences" in their growth. Some example pathologies are the Autism Spectrum Disorder (ASD), Down syndrome or Deafness. The professionals of these structures are mainly composed of Doctors, Therapists, Sociologists, and other specialists on the specific therapeutic for the tackled pathologies. Usually these structures are not equipped with dedicated technology experts or engineers that might help to create or develop ICT solutions that help the therapies.

Nevertheless, a literature review shows a clear benefit from the usage of technology in such therapies, namely the development of Digital Games, as mentioned in [1–3].

Giving the fact that this children audience is not the "mainstream", developing ICT solutions for this target does not attract as many big ICT enterprises as desired, exception made to some generic initiatives, e.g. in terms special interfaces for accessibility issues.

On the other hand side, some initiatives can be found in terms of collaboration between Universities and these kind of SCSs. These initiatives put together the efforts of the personnel from the SCSs, the Professors from the universities and usually some

C. Vaz de Carvalho et al. (Eds.): SGAMES 2015, LNICST 161, pp. 119–126, 2016.
DOI: 10.1007/978-3-319-29060-7_18

students, as well. Actually, the form of these partnerships divide the professionals from the SCSs and the professors from the universities as seniors that think about ICT systems or approaches that might improve some therapies, and the students as the juniors that design and develop such systems, usually as their final course project or master's dissertation *proof of concept* thesis prototype. In some cases, the developed prototypes are digital games, naturally, given their interaction means, as well as the entertainment aspect they bring to the therapies.

In these collaboration initiatives between Universities and SCSs, the students that finish their prototypes go to the final presentation and finish their courses, usually with a distinction for applying their learnings to concrete social targets. After that, they go to the next stage of their life. The result of this phase transition is that the prototype becomes orphan, meaning that no support may be provided, nor new versions developed according to some usage feedback. The consequence of this result is that although the prototype had received several credits, it will never become a product with a wide usage. In other words, it will not reach the final target users.

This paper proposes a new approach called Games' Social Tech Booster. The idea is to create a mechanism to apply technology to social issues through the games, based on the creativity, the technological know-how and enthusiasm from finalist students from ICT universities and, especially, guarantee the improvement of the prototypes that result from the partnerships, in order for them to really reach their target market.

2 State of the Art

The application of Games in health is not a new topic. In fact several serious games can be found in the industry, where the objective of the game is a serious aspect that is achieved through a gameplay that provides an entertainment and joyful environment where the player likes to be. Even some mainstream quite old games, like the Sid Meier's Civilization or the SimCity, provide the players with knowledge, e.g. in what concerns the Aztecs, or the organization of traffic, for the above mentioned examples.

In what concerns the production of games that target some examples of "differences" that children might have, some examples can be found as well. Depending on the size of the target audience, the number of existing games naturally increases.

A literature review organized by the pathologies children may have shows that one of the cases where the scientific community has put an interesting effort is the deafness. Some examples:

- American Sign Language recognition in game development for deaf children – [4] – A game that uses gesture recognition technology to help young deaf children practice American Sign Language skills.
- SMILE: an immersive learning game for deaf and hearing children – [5] – Science and Math in an Immersive Learning Environment), an immersive learning game that employs a fantasy 3D virtual environment to engage deaf and hearing children in math and science-based educational tasks.

- A gesture-based American Sign Language game for deaf children – [6] – A game designed to facilitate language development in deaf children for the American Sign Language.
- Kinect-Sign – [10] – A game devoted to teach the portuguese sign language to listeners.

Another example area that received much attention from the scientific community is the Autism Spectrum Disorder, as summarized in [11]. Some examples can also be found, like:

- [7] – Where a game was created for children diagnosed with autism spectrum disorder helping them to exercise face and objects recognition.
- [12] – Where a proposal is made towards providing expression recognition through a game.

In terms of technological devices' advances, some sensors appeared in the market, mainly devoted only to entertainment gamming, like the Kinect or the PlayStation sensors. These sensors have challenged researchers to use them with the focus of some of these child growth "differences", as well. Some efforts include:

- [8] – Where an extension to the kinect SDK was proposed towards recognizing gestures previuously saved.
- [9] – Where the kinect SDK was extended to include the hand skeleton added to the already existing body skeleton provided.

Although several other initiatives might be found, some contact with the doctors and therapists in the field shows that no sistematic approach exists and several other systems might be developped, as well. In other words, all these professionals thank the "ICT world", namelly in what concerns the adoption of games to complement the treatments they provide, but they feel the lack of dedicated ICT professionals to develop several other possible systems, i.e., there is a big potential application of ICT, especially in what concerns the digital games that target pathologies far from the mainstream.

In what concerns the University role and the above-mentioned collaboration innitiatives, as mentioned above, as the students proceed to the next stage of their lifes and leave an orphan prototype, the challenge is to overcome this aspect and, somehow, guarantee a continuation of these prototypes into the stage of products ready to reach their target market.

3 Games' Social Tech Booster

This paper proposes the concept called Games Social Tech Booster (GSTB), which is intended to become an enabler for the application of technology to social issues through games. The concept is based on students from Information and Communication Technology university courses, at their final year and especially afterwards.

The idea is to put together the energy and enthusiasm of these young students, or ex-students, the know-how of professionals from what we might call Beneficiary Organizations and University Professors. In terms of personnel organization, the GSTB will be made of seniors, the professors and the specialists from the Beneficiary Organizations; and juniors, some ex-students that will be hired after their final project or master's dissertation prototype is finished.

Moreover, a third and fourth potential GSTB partner kind is proposed: Finance support partners/Sponsors and Enterprises. Figure 1 represents all the potential partners from GSTB.

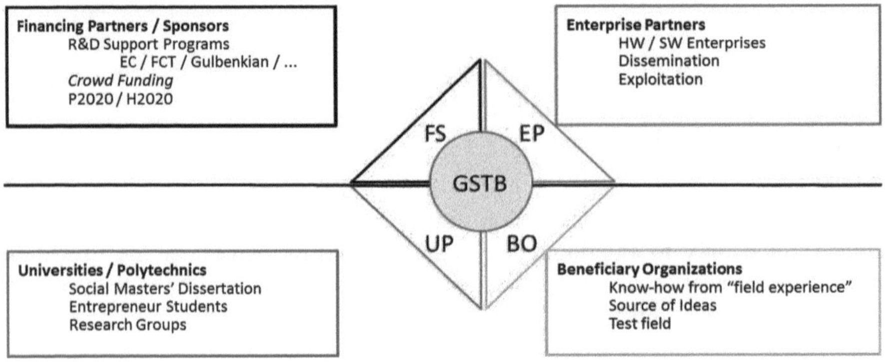

Fig. 1. Potential GSTB partners

As represented in Fig. 1, four distinct potential GSTB partner kinds were identified. At the baseline:

- Beneficiary Organizations – these are the structures created by the society to handle the social issues, which are equipped with doctors, therapists, etc. These structures are the source of the macro problem specifications. As they are the ones with the knowledge of the therapies and that deal with the children that will become the end-users of the games, they have the know-how of what are the main Needs.
- UP – Universities and Polytechnic – the Universities and Polytechnics are the labour source – the ex-students. As they have their final course projects, they provide topics for the finalist students to choose as their final course project, or masters' dissertation thesis, along with the beneficiary organizations. From the students' perspective, this will be an interesting option, especially if they have the willing to perform some sort of social work or if they have some entrepreneurship spirit.

These two potential partners are the baseline of the GSTB. Two other potential partners have also been identified:

- Financing Partners / Sponsors – As the main GSTB cost is the hiring of ex-students to transform their prototypes into products, the GSTB financing aspect becomes a core issue, as usual. Several potential financing entities were already identified. First, at a national level, several foundations were considered, as for example the Gulbenkian foundation or the EDP foundation, at the Portuguese national level. The Horizon 2020, at the European level and the corresponding Portugal 2020 have also been tackled in the perspective of applying R&D based on the GSTB concept.

- Enterprise Partners – finally, as the GSTB has an enterprise spirit, other enterprises were also identified as potential partners. Here HW and SW enterprises may contribute with their systems/games design and development know-how, but other enterprises will be needed for aspects like exploitation and dissemination, as well.

The proposed operational process is made of 4 phases and goes as follows: 1st, the Professionals from the Beneficiary Entities, along with the professors of the Universities identify projects that might be implemented towards helping therapists in their work. 2nd the finalist students that find such projects worth to implement, or that look at these projects and feel the enthusiasm or opportunity to apply their learnings to concrete social causes, apply for these projects and develop the expected prototype solutions. 3rd, the main GSTB phase, some of these students are hired to continue their prototypes towards improving them to become products. Finally, the products are deployed to the market through partner enterprises.

Figure 2 shows the 4 phases of the GSTB Business Model.

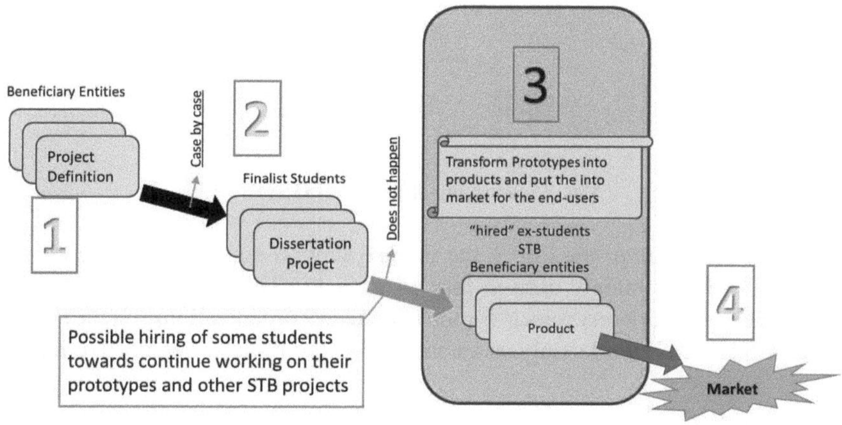

Fig. 2. GSTB business model

In other words, the process shown in Fig. 1, represents the Business Model of the GSTB, divided into 4 phases with the following roles:

1. <u>Idea / Need identification</u> – the first phase involves the GSTB itself and the Beneficiary Entities and targets the identification of the projects to be developed afterwards, as well as a macro-specification of such projects.
2. <u>Prototyping</u> – the second phase involves the GSTB, the University Professors and finalist students. This phase intends to perform the design and development of a prototype solution. This is a *proof of concept* prototype made for the student to finish his or her studies.
3. <u>"Productization"</u> – the third phase, the main GSTB aim, involves some ex-students, and the objective is to pick the developed prototype games and turn them into products towards reaching the final end-users. This final phase works in a cyclic manner, transforming the prototypes into products as mentioned, but also gathering the usage

experience feedback and transforming the products from one version in their next version, based on such feedback.

4. Deploy to market - Provide the market-ready products to partner enterprises that have the distribution channels ready to put the products in the market. After a time-frame, when the revenue starts being retrieved from the market, both the STB and the Beneficiary entities should benefit from it. The first needs to guarantee sustainability, the second owns part of the property rights.

Figure 3 represents the GSTB working structure in one picture.

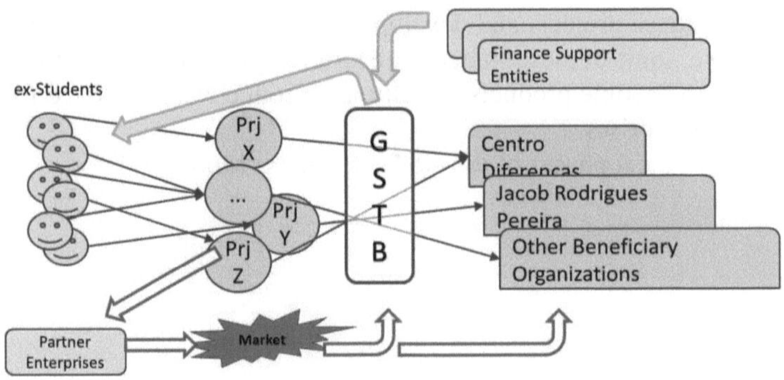

Fig. 3. Working structure of GSTB

At the top-right side of the Fig. 3, the finance support entities introduce the budget into the GSTB that is mainly used to hire ex-students. These ex-students (on the left hand-side of Fig. 3) work on projects for the beneficiary organizations (on the right-hand side). The GSTB itself works only as an enabler, as the Booster perspective induces.

4 Validation

The implementation of the STB concept has already started in the field with distinct prototypes already developed in collaboration with Beneficiary Organizations. Table 1 show some examples:

Table 1. Three sample projects already at the prototype stage.

Name	Short description	Benef. Org.
Kinect sign	Game devoted to teach Portuguese Sign Language to Listeners	Instituto Jacob Rodrigues Pereira (deaf children)
Game wizard	Wizard created to generate “Super-Mario”-like games through a user-friendly interface	Centro Diferenças
Reino dos Fonemas	Game created to teach phonemes to children with language learning difficulties.	Centro Diferenças

As shown in Table 1, two beneficiary organizations were tackled by these three sample projects. The GSTB idea is to work as a network of Polytechnics and Universities, as well as several Beneficiary Organizations. The already finished prototypes show that the distance between the prototype and the final products is not big and that the next stage of the GSTB itself is not difficult to achieve.

5 Conclusions and Future Work

The Games Social Tech Booster, proposed in this paper, intends to find a solution to guarantee the continuity of the prototypes designed and developed by finalist students as a result of the collaboration initiatives between Universities and the so called Beneficiary Organizations.

The main idea of this paper's proposal is not to introduce new forms for gamming nor new technologies, but rather to propose a new usage of existing knowledge from distinct areas that brought together might result I added value to the society. In other words, putting together the know-how of therapists, along with the enthusiasm of ICT finalist students with the orientation of their professors, may result games that help the therapy in several pathologies. GSTB proposes an approach to guarantee the evolution from the prototypes that result from the collaboration between Universities and Social Care Structures into products that really reach the end-users.

The concept of the GSTB have been presented, in the form of a Pitch, to distinct persons, from both Beneficiary Organizations, R&D Organizations and Research and Innovation Accelerators, as well as other backgrounds towards receiving inputs in what concerns the operational aspects and the philosophy of the concept. The acceptance is unanimous and the collaboration for the formation of a not-for-profit Association has already started.

In terms of future work, the network aspect has to grow, both involving other Universities and Polytechnics, as well as other Beneficiary Organizations.

The already involved BOs are providing macro project definitions and at the moment this paper is being written, 5 prototype systems are already finished and 4 are being designed and developed.

The concept was included in a Portugal 2020 proposal and more calls for proposals are being tackled. When the first financing success case occurs, ex-students will start to be hired and the operational "productization" process will start.

References

1. Wuang, Y.-P., Chiang, C.-S., Su, C.-Y., Wang, C.-C.: Effectiveness of virtual reality using Wii gaming technology in children. Res. Dev. Disabil. **32**(1), 312–321 (2011). Springer
2. Shane, H.C., Laubscher, E.H., Schlosser, R.W., Flynn, S., Sorce, J.F., Abramson, J.: Applying technology to visually support language and communication in individuals with autism spectrum disorders. J. Autism Dev. Disord. **42**(6), 1228–1235 (2012). Springer
3. Ploog, B.O., Scharf, A., DeShawn, N., Brooks, P.J.: Use of computer-assisted technologies (cat) to enhance social, communicative, and language development in children with autism spectrum disorders. J. Autism Dev. Disord. **43**(2), 301–322 (2013). Springer

4. Brashear, H., Henderson, V., Park, K.-H., Hamilton, H., Lee, S., Starner, T.: American sign language recognition in game development for deaf children. In: Proceedings of the 8th International ACM SIGACCESS Conference on Computers and Accessibility, pp 79–86. ACM, New York (2006)
5. Adamo-Villani, N., Wright, K.: SMILE: an immersive learning game for deaf and hearing children. In: Proceedings of ACM SIGGRAPH 2007 Educators Program, Article No. 17. ACM, New York (2007)
6. Lee, S., Henderson, V., Hamilton, H., Starner, T., Brashear, H., Hamilton, S.: A gesture-based american sign language game for deaf children. In: Proceedings of CHI 2005 Extended Abstracts on Human Factors in Computing Systems, pp 1589–1592. ACM, New York (2005)
7. Tanaka, J.W., Wolf, J.M., Klaiman, C., Koenig, K., Cockburn, J., Herlihy, L., Brown, C., Stahl, S., Kaiser, M.D., Schultz, R.T.: Using computerized games to teach face recognition skills to children with autism spectrum disorder: the Let's Face It! program. J. Child Psychol. Psychiatry **51**(8), 944–952 (2010)
8. Galveia, B., Carsoso, T., Rybarczyk, Y.: Adding value to the kinect SDK, creating a gesture library. EAI Endorsed Trans. Creative Technol. (2015). doi:10.4108/ct.2.3.e3
9. Cardoso, T., Delgado, J., Barata, J.: Hand gesture recognition towards enhancing accessibility. In: 6th International Conference on Software Development and Technologies for Enhancing Accessibility and Fighting Info-exclusion (2015)
10. Gameiro, J., Cardoso, T., Rybarczyk, Y.: Kinect-sign: teaching sign language to "listeners" through a game. In: Rybarczyk, Y., Cardoso, T., Rosas, J., Camarinha-Matos, L.M. (eds.) eNTERFACE 2013. IFIP AICT, vol. 425, pp. 141–159. Springer, Heidelberg (2014)
11. Grynszpan, O., Weiss, P.L., Perez-Diaz, F., Gal, E.: Innovative technology-based interventions for autism spectrum disorders: a meta-analysis. Autism **18**, 346–361 (2014)
12. Harrold, N., Tan, C.T., Rosser, D.: Towards an expression recognition game to assist the emotional development of children with autism spectrum disorders. In: WASA 2012 Proceedings of the Workshop at SIGGRAPH Asia, pp. 33–37. ACM, New York (2012)

BIM to IoT: The Persistence Problem

Steven Rowland(✉)

MSA, Stockholm, Sweden
steven.rowland@outlook.com

Abstract. This paper explores how gamification can provide the platform for integrating Building Information Modeling (BIM) together with the emergent Internet of Things (IoT). The goal of the research is to foster the creation of a testable and persistent virtual building via gaming technology that combines both BIM and IoT. The author discusses the features of each subject area in brief, and points towards the advantages and challenges of integration via gaming technology. Hospitals are the specific architectural typology discussed in the paper, as hospitals have particular properties which make them good candidates for study.

Keywords: BIM · IoT · Gamification · Buildings information model · Internet of things · AR · Augmented reality

1 Introduction

City Models have been tools of urban designers and city planners for centuries. A fine example is the Berlin Stadt Modelle museum, which maintains past and present scale models of the city of Berlin at various scales [1]. The Stadt Modelle is used for educating students about the past and present city by showing historical models, the divided city during the Cold War, and the present shaping of development along the former route Berlin Wall. Aside from the physical model, the Berlin urban authorities also maintain a CAD based 3D model, which is updated according to new development. Users of this model are limited to those who can use CAD formats, and therefore is not accessible to the general public.

Google Maps is a more accessible example, as complemented by its excellent Street View feature and 3-dimensional representations of many cities. Google Maps is complemented by GIS-powered Directions features. Many other HTTP-based information sources are available through web-links. The interiors of buildings are mostly inaccessible (with a few exception), limiting the 3-dimensional shapes of buildings and cityscape to representational rather than informational in most cases. Google Maps has even been experienced as virtual reality by using Street View via Oculus Rift [2]. The limitation, again, is that it is representational, and buildings in Street View are little more than panoramic photographs burned onto geometry as a texture.

This paper proposes, instead, an informational city model with the following features:

C. Vaz de Carvalho et al. (Eds.): SGAMES 2015, LNICST 161, pp. 127–137, 2016.
DOI: 10.1007/978-3-319-29060-7_19

1. Building Information Model imbued geometry
2. Real-Time data via the Internet of Things
3. Multiplayer Online Gaming based platform
4. Augmented Reality Interface

The paper will discuss each of these areas briefly in turn, and then summarize the advantages of an informational city model, as BIM-IoT Game is being proposed.

2 Why BIM Matters

Building Information Modelling (BIM) is a design process that is used in current architecture practice to describe, model, and publish the documentation required for constructing buildings, structures and urban design in general. There are a variety of BIM platforms, however BIM is not a single specific software. Rather it is the total information, spatial, and aesthetic design of "something" (typically a building) that can be spread across a variety of software and datatypes. The goal of BIM is always the same: create the comprehensive documentation required to build something efficiently [3].

2.1 Features of BIM

BIM models are parametric; meaning that parameters are used to control and contain the design information and spatial forms. BIM platforms are in fact advanced 3-dimensional, visual, database systems that combine aesthetics with documentation, change management, analysis, space planning, etc. etc. etc. It is difficult to describe the totality of BIM, but suffice to say that BIM is the modern practice of architecture. An entire new discipline of building professional, the BIM manager, has grown from the prevalence of BIM methodology.

BIM can be described as a top-down process. This is not particular to BIM, but architectural design has always been top-down discipline. Example: Building developers describe the requirements and intentions, Architects design and describe those requirements via BIM, and Builders construct the physical building according to the documentation and information transmitted via the BIM model. This is not to say that architecture is not inclusive of many perspectives; in fact the modern practice employs wide teams of experts, community members, sociologists, and political voices. Nevertheless, the structure is overall hierarchal and thereby can be described as top-down.

If we consider an entire city over time, then the overall built environment can be considered bottom-up, with many and varied actors creating the city. Individual buildings, however, are almost invariably top-down.

2.2 Why BIM Matters

Information has always been the essence of Architectural design. Whether an architect draws by hand or via AutoCAD or Revit, the eternal purpose has been to encode information in drawings, notations, and other documents for describing something to be built.

BIM has elevated information and data management to a central role and freed architectural data from the confines of paper. Leading BIM platform typically have a level of openness that invites further development and creativity via Accessible Programming Interfaces (API). BIM matters not only because it is the status quo among leading architectural practices, but also because the open data structure allows us to grow beyond the limitations of any particular software. The API and programming community around BIM has grown substantially and continues to accelerate. Coding has become a highly valuable skill for architecture.

The BIM model itself has become a standard deliverable for many projects, at times supplanting drawings entirely. The once all-important printer has been relegated to the status of a legal requirement and source of irritations relating to toner and paper jams. BIM has also become a mandated standard for government projects in certain countries and types of projects, notably in the UK. Various developers have also mandated BIM standards, as they perceive that it delivers a superior product and pathway to life-cycle facilities management.

2.3 The Value of the BIM

The BIM model is encoded with valuable information, but that value may be perceived differently by different stakeholders. For example, regional healthcare authorities want to know the number of trauma wards for regional emergency planning, while waste disposal contractors want to know the number and location of waste containers for estimating disposal costs and logistics for removal. An artist wants to understand the spatial qualities of the space where he/she has been awarded a commissioned. Herein lies the problem; different actors could benefit from the BIM data in different ways, and most likely in ways that are unpredictable. Only one actor, however, owns the data directly and thereby acts as a gatekeeper.

Ownership of the BIM data is often quite clear: The building owner usually has sole ownership over the totality of the BIM model and the information contained therein as it pertains to that specific building or thing. Some BIM-derived information would be extracted as legal documents at various points in the design and approval process (permit drawings, traffic approvals), but ongoing access to the BIM model is typically controlled solely by the ownership organization or its proxies.

We don't treat our buildings BIM data in the same way that we treat GIS data, which, in western democracies, is generally much more open to creative analysis. BIM data, as with the physical buildings themselves, are private. More often than not, the BIM data is largely discarded at the conclusion of production.

2.4 What BIM Can Offer to IoT

We have all by now heard about the Internet of Things (IoT), and we are all mostly confused by what the fuss is all about. What we can say is that internet connected devices can create an ambient flow of information via internet protocols, which can be made useful by thoughtful applications. IoT nodes includes things like traffic lights, which when internet connected can provide both instant traffic feedback as well as histories of data to be analyzed later. Other nodes are less obvious, such as sensors embedded in waste receptacles that can signal when they become full. The single instances are mostly insignificant, but the sum of IoT enabled devices provides a powerful source of information that can be harnessed to provide efficiency and intelligence.

As opposed to the top down implementation of BIM, the Internet of Things is a bottom up, emergent phenomenon. Individual nodes can be added or subtracted, and assuming the protocols are all standard, the IoT cluster expands or contracts automatically. It is comparable to a group of huddling penguins on a frozen beach somewhere; individual penguins can wander off or return from a swim, but the Internet of Penguin ™ remains as long as two of the odd birds remain to continue clucking at each other.

The internet of things is built on the foundation of *horizontal information silos* that carry information across and between the individual islands of data. Currently BIM is a vertical information silo that can offer very specific information about the built environment, that which is visible as well as the invisible. Again we can think of all the parts of a building as nodes within a system, in much the same way that IoT devices can be considered as nodes of the IoT ecosystem. Examples of visible nodes includes things like the structure of a wall, the manufacturer of a floor covering, or the system capacity of a cooling tower. Invisible nodes are more conceptual, like a room or a space, which has no physical presence, but nevertheless carries a large amount of information. It is the marriage of visible and invisible nodes that makes the BIM model such a useful tool and source of information.

2.4.1 Context

"Where am I?" is a common question that we answer every day with applications like Google Maps. GPS systems like TomTom help us find our location when we drive in unfamiliar places. When we arrive at a building, however, we tend to leave that concept behind us. The owner of the building may provide signs to aid in way-finding, and rooms may have signs that say where they are. The interior arrangement of a building is generally considered to be private and in many cases secure. Government buildings are careful that the location of offices for important officials are not accessible to the general public, for example.

There are many buildings that are considered more public, and could benefit from more open and connected forms of way-finding. For example a shopping mall benefits from having the stores discoverable for visitors. A visitor to a hospital complex is sometimes mystified by the layout. This is compounded when a visitor is wanting to find a sick or injured loved-one, which can understandably create anxiety when the visitor is confused by the building layout. This is a great example of where the BIM model can be paired with IoT to answer the question of where is the patient's room (BIM), and where is the specific patient right now (IoT).

2.4.2 Requirements

Rooms have specific requirements related to their function. For example, a recording studio has specific acoustic requirements, a datacenter server hall has specific humidity levels, and an operating theatre has required hygienic levels. Room requirements are managed via Room Objects in a BIM model, the rooms as objects are otherwise invisible conceptual spaces in a building, but are the centers of information flow in a BIM model.

A BIM model can therefore answer questions of the intentions of rooms as according to the design of the room. A radio-medical technician can thereby know instantly if the room has the correct radiation shielding for a new piece of equipment if the BIM data is accessible in real time via IoT.

2.4.3 Spatial Awareness

BIM models describe spaces and the things that define the spaces, like walls, ceilings, floors etc. At a very basic level, BIM-IoT can deliver information like area or volume, but it can also deliver 3-dimensional visualization, and the relationship or connections between spaces. Spatial information in a BIM-IoT deployment can be visualized either in the building or remotely. Training scenarios can be much more immersive for planning evacuation, security, logistics, or orientation.

2.4.4 The Promise of Persistence

Persistence is defined as the continued or prolonged existence of something. A persistent online game is where the game world continues after the local game user has ended their session. Other players are still using the persistent online game world, and significant actions can occur which will alter the local users game after the session is continued again.

A persistent BIM-IoT keeps the BIM model alive after local users have ceased to access it. A persistent BIM imbued with IoT promises the ability for multiple users at different times to access both the device ecosystem pulsing through the built environment as well as access to the design intentions, design data (what is that wall made of?), and spatial qualities. Myriad other aspects of the BIM model can give deep context to the real-time IoT nodes.

If the top-down BIM model is to be synthesized with the bottom-up IoT ecosystem, then the building owner has to solve the problem of persistence. Simply put, how is the BIM-IoT hybrid kept alive? What is the format the effectively represents the potential of these two technologies? What skills are required to create and maintain the BIM-IoT hybrid? What is the revenue model that maintains BIM-IoT? What is the payback period?

3 Why Games Matter

3.1 Persistence

The Multiuser Online Game (MOG) has become a dominant paradigm for many big-budget games. Almost all AAA games released from major games studios in recent times have an online component that allows players from across the globe to compete in a virtual world. More often than not these are first-person shooter type games (Call of Duty). There are several subgenres under the rubric MOG, but the common thread is an internet based game through which multiple (sometimes thousands) of players can interact in a highly detailed world simultaneously. MOG games persist after single players have left, as other players continue to compete, cooperate, or explore the online world.

3.2 Immersion

Games take a wide variety of forms, but for this discussion I will focus on the first-person shooter variety (minus the shooter). First-Person Games take the point-of-view of the player themselves. By employing mouse, keyboard or controller manipulation, the player navigates a 3-d world and often completes tasks or defeats enemies. The point-of-view is the key to creating a sense of immersion and presence in the 3D world. A player that feels immersion can achieve a higher level of motivation to compete, explore, and play the game to its conclusion.

3.3 Fun

Games, on some level, are designed to be fun. To paraphrase (from something entirely different), "I don't know what fun is, but I know it when I am having it". Fun is difficult to define, but in the context of games it can be attempting to solve a difficult puzzle, battling across an arena, exploring a vast world, or any number of different variations that someone, somewhere thinks is fun. A key feature of being fun is that the game mechanics, that is the controls, the rules, the interface, are not so cumbersome or ergonomically difficult as to interfere with the actual game play. For a game to be fun, the user interface and user experience should probably be intuitive, stable, and perhaps even beautiful on some level. Further delving into the idea of fun can lead to very complicated philosophical abstractions, and I don't think this paper needs to go there. I will leave it this way: There is a thing called fun, people know when they are having fun, and generally people want to keep having more fun. That last component, the desire to have more fun, is the most important aspect. Fun is enticing, inviting, and approachable. Fun turns work into a game. Fun is motivating.

3.4 Complexity

Scientific research has already made the jump to gamification in some examples. The Wellcome Trust Sanger Institute in 2013 teamed up with Epic Games, the makers of Unreal Engine, to sponsor a competition to create games around the theme of "Mendelian inheritance: genetics and genomics". "There's something about genetics that seems to lend itself to computer games," said Carl Anderson, a researcher at the Wellcome Trust Sanger Institute [4].

4 A New Approach: Gamification of BIM-IoT

A variety of services has been delivering BIM to gaming platforms. Some notable examples are Revizto, Lumion3d, and Twinmotion. Revizto aims to aid in project collaboration during the design and construction process, while Lumion3d and Twinmotion are high-end rendering platforms that leverage gaming technology.

Apart from the services and others on the market already, architects are able to export BIM models directly into gaming platforms themselves. Popular and powerful game engines such as Unity or Unreal Engine are being used in current architectural practice to create game-like environments for client walkthroughs, prototyping, and virtual reality experiments. Visualization specialists in architecture are increasingly offering to translate architectural and real estate proposals into high-end gaming platforms.

More importantly, it is possible with available technique to retain the BIM data when published in the game environment. I have a large healthcare project being designed currently, where BIM Gaming is being applied to the design review and visualization process via Revizto. This is been received very enthusiastically by our clients. Gamification of BIM has allowed architectural clients to interact with the BIM design in a very approachable, immersive, fun format.

The Gaming industry has solved many of the most challenging aspects of presenting complex environments in a first-person game. Think of any of the more recent AAA games released by major studios, with an eye towards the complexity of the game. Furthermore, gaming technology via Multiplayer Online Games has solved the persistence problem of online environments. Richly detailed MOGs like World of Warcraft or EVE are persistent and accessed concurrently by millions of players. BIM-IoT Gaming can shed many of the complex game mechanics of MOGs, and retain the persistent world aspect and level loading technologies.

4.1 Overlaying the Real with the Unreal

In the paper "A Multiplayer Learning Game based on Mixed Reality to Enhance Awareness on Archaeology" researchers used a multiplayer online game to increase immersion, motivation, and effectiveness of archaeology education [5]. Mixed reality scenarios took students out of the game to investigate real life artefacts. This example uses is very close to the scenario I am proposing, however BIM-IoT Gaming uses the real buildings and the real city complemented with real-time IoT data.

The concept of overlaying the real and unreal has been defined as *Pervasive Games* [6], where "Pervasive Gaming implies the construction and enacting of augmented and/or embedded game worlds that reside on the threshold between tangible and immaterial space, which may further include adaptronics, embedded software, and information systems in order to facilitate a 'natural' environment for game play that ensures the explicitness of computational procedures in a post-screen setting" [7].

4.2 Augmented Reality

Augmented Reality interfaces are the most promising candidates for experiencing the merged BIM and IoT game system. In previous literature this has been dubbed Mixed Reality [8], and it refers to a merging of virtual and actual worlds. Recent examples have included Google Glass, and promising prototypes like Microsoft HoloLens technology. Hypothetical examples are Magic Leap, which has not yet disclosed the hardware, software, or indeed much else of their AR applications beyond a few videos. Other very successful AR solutions are the Osterhout Group, who have been making sophisticated AR glasses for the American military, and plan to release consumer AR glasses in 2015. Some might question why we would overlay a virtual building onto a real building. What's the point, when I can just tap on a real wall to know that, yes, it is a concrete wall?

The pervasive overlay, accessed via AR allows the ability to know the structure of the wall. Does this wall have sufficient radiation shielding? What is behind this wall? Where are the heating ducts located behind the wall? Microsoft showed an excellent example of this, where the Hololens allowed the ability to blast a virtual hole in a real wall and view a Minecraft world beyond. With AR a maintenance worker could dematerialize a wall to find the mechanical or plumbing systems inside.

The ideal BIM-IoT Game would be accessible in a variety of ways, including via mobile phones, laptops and desktops. Different access formats invariably requires a different range of capabilities. Desktop and laptops could have very advanced analytical capabilities through APIs that are not generally possible in a mobile or AR deployment.

4.3 The Hypothetical Hospital

Hospitals are a great test-case for this technology because they are typically complex spatially, extremely information dense, and having very high concentrations of equipment which could be IoT enabled. Healthcare equipment manufacturers like Siemens are amongst the leaders in IoT technology, as is an indication of the coming integration of IoT sensors in hospital equipment. Furthermore, hospitals have a wide cross section of users who all experience the buildings very differently.

Let's take a stroll through the Hypothetical Hospital to illustrate how BIM-IoT Gaming might be experienced: A visitor comes to the hospital to visit a patient. She has received an email with her relative's room number, and she registers herself as a visitor. When she arrives at the hospital she is presented with turn-by-turn directions in her AR glasses to find her relative's room. This is also complemented by virtual and physical way-finding signs. Her relative, the patient, is being taken for a test in another part of the hospital, and an update alert is sent. The Visitor can either follow a new set of turn-by-turn or continue following directions to a waiting area. A logistics worker receives an alert from an IoT enabled sensor in Just-In-Time cabinet outside a surgery. New surgical gowns need to be delivered. He checks out the goods from Sterilization Central and delivers them to the exact cabinet, which can be identified further via AR highlighting. A maintenance worker receives an alert from an IoT enabled ventilation fan that a part is failing. He gets the replacement part and goes to the room. He dematerializes the wall in his AR vision, and overlays the equipment in his view. He calls the ventilation specialist for detailed instructions on replacing the part. The ventilation specialist shares the camera view. An A/V technician is hanging a new monitor on a wall. He checks the wall's structure via the BIM overlay to ensure that there is plywood where she wants to install the new monitor. There is no need to tear open the wall to check. A hospital administrator sees the need for more intensive care rooms. She logs into the BIM-IoT game on her laptop and analyzes the hygienic class of the existing nearby rooms to plan the possible changes. A patient is going to undergo emergency surgery. An expert surgeon in another country is assisting remotely. The Surgeon in the operating room can see an avatar of the existing surgeon who is giving detailed instructions. The assisting surgeon can see and access the equipment in the room and feel immersed in the room spatially. An artist is invited to create an installation for the children's ward. He uses the 3-d BIM model to understand the space and creates a virtual representation in the actual space. The hospital arts director visits the children's ward, and sees via AR the proposed installation layered over on the actual space, and shows the AR model to children and staff in the ward for feedback.

5 Conclusions

Often innovative ideas are birthed in speculative fiction of one sort or another. For example, William Gibson predicted much of the potential for the gamification of BIM-IoT in his Virtual Light novel, or the tablet computer was visualized in Kubrick's 2001: a Space Odyssey. Other technology seems nearly achieved, such as the communicators of Star Trek, or the space elevator theorized by Arthur C Clarke. Complications for this proposal include:

- Miniaturization: Current AR technology is too big and cumbersome for the average consumer to use daily. Hololens is a large visor, while Magic Leaps theoretical hardware prototypes have been described as very cumbersome at this point. The Osterhout Group's glasses are the closest to "normal" sunglasses, but even those are not exactly fashionable. AR technology has a long road ahead until it can be miniaturized sufficiently to deliver an acceptable form factor for mass acceptance in the consumer market.
- Patching the game: Fortunately, the games industry has solved the problem of updating their games through patches and downloadable content (DLC). A similar patching procedure could keep the BIM-IoT model updated as new buildings come online, and new IoT equipment is introduced. Who is responsible for upkeep? Is it an emergent system, where patching is handled in a decentralized way, or is a central authority responsible? Perhaps it could be both, for different levels of information.
- Revenue and payback: In general, building owners use very short term formulas when valuing payback for additions to the basic objective of the building. A 3 to 5 year payback period can be an acceptable target. BIM-IoT would almost certainly require higher design fees, and may add operation costs if updates to the underlying BIM model is required. New revenue streams are one way to achieve acceptance, for example microtransactions from users, telecommunication fees, or even advertising in the virtual space. In the retail space, the introduction of a new dimension to sales and advertising could be a valuable new type of payback.
- Security and propriety (Hackers): Some information about the interiors and data in buildings should be always be kept secure. The locations of vital systems, valuables, and people is clearly very sensitive information that should be controlled carefully. The example of Anders Breivik's attack on the Oslo offices of the Norwegian government illustrates this in the extreme. Systems need to have robust informational

security to block access. None of this is particular to BIM-IoT, but is a dimension that would need to be carefully considered. The evolution of the sophisticated hacker has shown that even the most isolated systems can be hacked.
- Proprietary information: The vast majority of buildings are privately owned, and the interiors of private buildings are by definition proprietary. The typical building owner has no requirement for opening their building to the virtual, and probably only a small fraction of private building owners would even entertain the idea of an open BIMIoT Game. However, we can consider the evolution of GPS and aerial photography as an example where the previously inaccessible was suddenly wide open for scrutiny. The satellite view in mapping services is taken for granted now, but at its dawn was the feeling that the world was being revealed at a level of detail previously only visible to national militaries. A similar evolution of public-private could occur in BIM-IoT gamification.
- Evolution of the contract: Currently, building owners are required to submit building permit drawings and certain zoning diagrams with supporting documentation. In the fully realized BIM-IoT cityscape, it would be conceivable that municipal authorities would require suitable BIM models. Designers, architects, and engineers also would need a revised contract that details the new type of deliverable. A BIM model limited to production can be very different than a BIM model that is targeted towards production and life-cycle BIM-IoT gamification. New standards could be required to help achieve acceptable levels of detail, and new subcategories of professionals could be necessary for creating and servicing the BIM-IoT Game.

I'm embarrassed to say that this paper was inspired by an episode of CSI, where the Crime Scene Investigators accessed a detailed 3d model of an existing building, complete with real-time information from building systems. As an architect I knew that this kind of persistent virtual building was nonsense at the time, and I have seen many examples of the same concept presented in various other shows and even cartoons. As an architect, I enjoy seeing the designs that we create become actual parts of the built environment. The actualization of architecture is one of the most gratifying aspects of the profession. What is less satisfying is the fate of the BIM model. Architects will spends months or years on the BIM models, only to see them largely discarded at the end of production. My intuition tells me there is more value to be delivered to our clients, our cities, and the people inhabiting it. The trend of technology and our information society tells me that BIM-IoT is coming in one form or another, and Gamification is the way forward.

References

1. Berlin Stadt Modelle. http://www.stadtentwicklung.berlin.de/planen/stadtmodelle/de/ausstellung.shtml
2. Oculus Street View. http://oculusstreetview.eu.pn/
3. National BIM Standard – United States. http://www.nationalbimstandard.org/faq.php#faq1
4. Wellcome Trust Blog, The science of gaming: 'Make Something Unreal Live'. http://blog.wellcome.ac.uk/2013/02/21/the-science-of-gaming-make-something-unreal-live/

5. Loiseau, M., Lavoué, E., Marty, J.-C., George, S.: A multiplayer learning game based on mixed reality to enhance awareness on archaeology. SG ICST (2014). doi:10.4108/sg.1.3.e3
6. Hinske, S., Lampe, M., Magerkurth, C., Röcker, C.: Classifying pervasive games: on pervasive computing and mixed reality. Institute for Pervasive Computing, ETH Zurich, Switzerland (2007). http://www.coulthard.com/library/Files/hinske_2007_classifyingpervasivegames.pdf
7. Walther, B.K.: Atomic actions & molecular experience: theory of pervasive gaming. ACM Comput. Entertainment **3**, 4 (2005)
8. Milgram, P., Kishino, F.: A taxonomy of mixed reality visual displays. IEICE Trans. Inf. Syst. **E77-D**(12), 1321–1329 (1994)

Author Index

MIX
Papier aus verantwortungsvollen Quellen
Paper from responsible sources
FSC® C105338

If you have any concerns about our products,
you can contact us on
ProductSafety@springernature.com

In case Publisher is established outside the EU,
the EU authorized representative is:
Springer Nature Customer Service Center GmbH
Europaplatz 3, 69115 Heidelberg, Germany

Printed by Libri Plureos GmbH
in Hamburg, Germany